DABO'S WORLD

ALSO BY LARS ANDERSON

DABO'S WORLD

THE LIFE AND CAREER OF COACH SWINNEY AND THE RISE OF CLEMSON FOOTBALL

LARS ANDERSON

GRAND CENTRAL
PUBLISHING

NEW YORK   BOSTON

Grand Central Publishing
Hachette Book Group
1290 Avenue of the Americas, New York, NY 10104
grandcentralpublishing.com
twitter.com/grandcentralpub

First Edition: October 2021

Grand Central Publishing is a division of Hachette Book Group, Inc. The Grand Central Publishing name and logo is a trademark of Hachette Book Group, Inc.

The publisher is not responsible for websites (or their content) that are not owned by the publisher.

The Hachette Speakers Bureau provides a wide range of authors for speaking events. To find out more, go to www.hachettespeakersbureau.com or call (866) 376-6591.

Library of Congress Control Number: 2021939217

ISBNs: 978-1-5387-5343-9 (hardcover), 978-1-5387-5344-6 (ebook)

Printed in the United States of America

LSC-C

Printing 1, 2021

For Erik Robert Anderson,
my best friend,
my brother

Commitment is what transforms a
promise into reality.

—Abraham Lincoln

CONTENTS

CONTENTS

DABO'S WORLD

CHAPTER 1

RUN, DABO, RUN

There he was, alone in his South Carolina hotel room suite at the Hilton Garden Inn, alone with his coaching notes, alone at a desk, his head buried under the amber glow of lamplight. Over the previous quarter century, he had scribbled countless concepts and diagrams and coaching thoughts on pieces of paper that he had stored in folders and three-ring binders, and he dug through his most important pieces of information one more time at the hotel in the town of Anderson. A defining hour of his young life was fast approaching.

Throughout the day, he had projected an image of confidence and strength—during morning meetings with coaches, his afternoon interactions with players, his exchanges with fans—but now in his suite, surrounded by silence on the evening of October 17, 2008, his heart thumped, a jackhammer pounding inside of his chest. His first game as interim head coach of the Clemson Tigers was slated to kick off the next afternoon, and at this moment, as darkness fell outside his hotel window, Dabo Swinney was a mess of nerves.

A planner's planner, Dabo believed he was ready for his head-coaching debut. Just that night at the team hotel—after he had spoken to his players in a ballroom and told them how much he cared for them and loved them—he felt that his offense and defense and special teams were prepared to play at a high level against Georgia Tech. He knew that his well-thought-out pregame speech, one that he had been fine-tuning and waiting his entire coaching life—twenty-five years—to deliver, contained all the fire and passion and inspiration of a preacher in a Southern pulpit.

But the one thing Dabo hadn't practiced now *really* worried him: He had never run down the grassy, steep—and often slippery—hill in the east end zone of Memorial Stadium, a pregame tradition for the players at Clemson's home field. As an assistant coach, Dabo had always walked onto the field through a different entrance with the other assistants, so he wasn't fully aware of any invisible booby traps that awaited him, especially because he would be wearing smooth-soled shoes rather than cleats like his players.

No head coach in Clemson history had ever led his players down that deep green grassy slope, but then again, Dabo was different. He wanted to show the fans his excitement, his passion, his love of the game, and his belief in the power of a singular possibility—that he was the one who would lead the Tiger program, literally and figuratively, to the summit of college football. Yet here he was, fearful of losing his footing and tumbling down the hill, becoming a low-light reel blooper, a football klutz, not to mention a living symbol of the beginning of his tenure at Clemson, which many in coaching circles and in the national media believed was destined to fail. Heck, few outside of Clemson, South Carolina, had ever heard of this thirty-eight-year-old head coach with the quirky first name, a man who had never even been a coordinator for a football team before.

Just seven years earlier, he was out of football and working as a shopping center leasing agent in Birmingham, Alabama, talking traffic patterns and demographics and anchor stores with potential customers. Then Tommy Bowden hired him to coach the wide receivers at Clemson in 2003 and now— improbably—he was elevated to interim head coach when Bowden stepped down after a humbling 12–7 loss to Wake Forest. How rare was it for a position coach to become an interim head coach and then ascend to permanent head coach? Think of Halley's Comet streaking across the heavens: about once every seventy-five years.

Oh my God, thought Swinney in his hotel room on the eve of his first game, *I'm going to have to run down that hill in front of eighty-five thousand people and a bunch of people with TV cameras tomorrow.* Yes, ready or not, Swinney's moment of reckoning on that hill was coming.

DABO SWINNEY HAD BEEN named interim head coach six days earlier on October 13, 2008, and he wanted his players to experience the intoxicating thrill of game day even before they reached the stadium. When he was an assistant, Dabo spent many Saturday mornings before kickoff meeting with recruits in a building away from the stadium. Once these meet and greets were over, he'd stroll through the parking lots, chocka-block with orange-clad fans tailgating from pop-up tents and cars and pickup trucks with Clemson flags sprouting from the flatbeds. Underneath the tents emblazoned with Tiger paws, fans grilled burgers and wings, tossed footballs and Frisbees, and sipped adult beverages. The atmosphere was electric—the sights, the smells, and the sounds overwhelmed Dabo's senses—and that always jolted the assistant coach, spreading a pinch-me smile across his face, filling him with the belief that he was the luckiest dadgum man alive, one who had the best job in America, surrounded every autumn Saturday by the pomp and pageantry and poetry of college football. Now Dabo was determined to have his players feel— really *feel, deep down*—the full-body shiver of emotions that he always enjoyed during these pregame walks through the parking lots.

So after becoming interim head coach, Dabo called a meeting in his office with the state troopers who escorted the team buses from the football facility to the stadium on game days. Under Bowden and every other Clemson coach, the buses that ferried the players to the stadium had avoided traffic by taking a circuitous route using rural roads. But Dabo was adamant: He wanted the buses to drive through the middle of campus, through the beating heart of the tailgating fans, so his players could understand how the game was so important to so many. The team had often played lifeless, listless football through the first half of the 2008 season—a who-really-cares attitude had infected the roster and was a major reason why Bowden was no longer the head coach—and Dabo wanted his players to experience the heat of the fans' passion, to let it wash over them and, he hoped, inspire them to play the game of their lives.

At first the state troopers and others in the administration balked at the suggestion, explaining to Dabo that rerouting the buses would create a traffic nightmare. The young interim head coach, who eventually spread out a map on his desk and kept pointing at the campus roads he wanted the buses to travel on, stood his ground. "Y'all are not listening to me," Dabo said. "You want to win this game? We are not going that way...I need these guys to see the whole pageantry of Clemson."

There was more. Dabo told the bus drivers to park a few hundred yards away from the entrance of the locker room. For years the buses had simply pulled up to the door and the players—outfitted in sweat suits or whatever casual apparel they felt like wearing (most also with headphones on)—simply strolled inside, unbothered and unseen by fans.

No longer, said Dabo. This was his regime: The buses would stop at Lot 5 on Perimeter Road and the players would walk 200 yards through a cluster of screaming, high-fiving fans, providing the shot of adrenaline the entire program needed. What was more, Dabo mandated that his players wear a coat and tie. He also banned headphones, because his players needed to absorb the rush of sensory overload he had enjoyed on his game-day walks across the lots. Dabo instituted these rules to underscore to his players the specialness and seriousness of the occasion. He called this event the Tiger Walk. The reason for creating it was clear: He wanted his players to internalize the excitement and joy and fervor of the fans, to fully understand that they were playing for something that was far bigger than themselves or even their team.

Does all this really matter when it comes to winning football games? In Dabo's World, yes.

ABOUT TWENTY MINUTES BEFORE noon on October 18, 2008, Dabo slid into what would become his normal seat on the lead bus—row 1, seat 1—and gazed out the window as the wheels began to roll. To enter the stadium by running down the hill, the head coach and the players rode buses from the locker room to the east end zone. It was a short ride, only a few minutes, but what a moment this was for Dabo. Outside, late-arriving fans were still streaming through the gates for the noontime kickoff against Georgia Tech, but not even the most ardent Clemson backers knew exactly how far Dabo had come to reach this point.

His alcoholic father could be abusive, and Dabo spent many nights as a kid in Pelham, Alabama, sleeping in a car with his mom or sitting on the roof of his house waiting for the yelling and banging inside to stop. He was a walk-on at Alabama, making the roster as a slow-footed, overachieving wide receiver, eventually winning a national championship ring as a member of Alabama's 1992 team. Money was so tight during college that his mother lived with him and a roommate in an apartment in Tuscaloosa—Dabo and his mom even shared a bed—and on many weekends when he didn't have football responsibilities, Dabo would drive forty-five minutes to wealthy neighborhoods in Birmingham to clean gutters to make a few extra dollars.

The lead bus rolled closer to the east end zone entrance, and Dabo's pulse quickened. His dream was unfolding, but as he stepped off the bus, his thoughts quickly turned to what had bothered him the night before: How was he going to get down that hill? If he fell, he knew he'd become a national joke, and even worse, he'd likely be trampled by his players following in his wake, a mass of very large people that could flatten him with startling efficiency and speed, a herd of thundering humans that could stomp the air and life out of a five-foot-eleven middle-aged man.

Dabo emerged at the top of the hill in front of his players, raising his arms in the air, the crowd cheering. He peered down the hill, realizing it looked steeper now than he had ever imagined. His players behind him were whooping and hollering, but Dabo could only think about how he would have to navigate the grassy, rapid descent in front of him. He focused on his feet. *Pick them up and put them down,* he thought. *Just pick them up and put them down.* He looked back out to the crowd and was so caught up in the moment inside Memorial Stadium—also called "Death Valley"—that he bent over and kissed Howard's Rock, a large piece of white flint imported from the actual Death Valley in California that players touch for good luck before they run onto the field. Watching from the stands, Dabo's mom, Carol, recoiled at the sight of her son planting a wet one on the rock that had been touched by so many, thinking of the germs imparted to his lips.

Then a cannon fired, and Dabo took off at full speed, full throttle—no half-assing it now—running like his shoelaces were on fire, sprinting like no coach in Clemson history had done before a game. Stride after stride, he smiled and looked like he was a kid in a footrace, as if he was back in the front yard of his childhood home in Alabama, trying to beat his buddies as they ran from the mailbox to a maple tree. Stride after stride, he gained speed, his players chasing him down the hill. Seeing their coach take off like a Thoroughbred out of the gate, the crowd whipped itself into a boiling froth, producing a roar of noise that resounded several blocks before being swallowed by a brilliant blue autumn sky. Once he reached the field, Dabo's legs kicked into another gear, and he now ran like he was again a player at Alabama going deep to snare a long ball from his old quarterback Jay Barker.

Dabo sped across the goal line, the 10-, the 20-, the 30-yard line, still at full sprint. Oh, what a scene this was, the fans in a full-throated frenzy, their coach showing so much joy and spirit and excitement on the field. He wasn't a coach down there on the field; he was a young man having the time of his life, showing everyone in the stands that even though he may have looked silly, he didn't care. All that mattered—all that would ever matter to Dabo—was that when he did something, he did it 100 percent, all in with no regrets, and he was going to do it with childlike exhilaration and animation. It was a living example of one of Dabo's favorite phrases: *How you do anything is how you do everything.* For Dabo, this meant going all out, all the time, no matter the circumstances, no matter the score, no matter who was watching.

At the 40-yard line, Dabo kept running through the bright fall sunshine, his legs pumping like pistons. Cheerleaders marched toward the midfield as the band played the Clemson fight song—and Dabo ran past them all. Once he finally stopped, the young coach turned and high-fived his players, jumping up and down, encouraging them, telling them that this was their moment, their time, their game. Fans continued to raise a roar that rolled like thunder through the cool Southern sky.

This was only a moment that lasted a few seconds, but let's freeze time here and soak it in, because only in retrospect can we see how important it was, how it revealed the fundamental essence of Dabo Swinney. In his first public appearance at Memorial Stadium as the head coach of the Clemson Tigers, it became clear he believed—truly believed—that anything in life and football could be conquered as long as you are willing to take a chance on yourself.

THERE HE WAS, MOVING up and down the sideline at Wake Forest, a ball of kinetic energy, striding from player to player and coach to coach, talking to them, encouraging them, advising them. It was the evening of September 12, 2020, the season opener against the Demon Deacons, and with less than ninety seconds remaining in the first half, quarterback Trevor Lawrence connected with J.C. Chalk on a 12-yard touchdown pass to give the Tigers a 24–0 lead. The score prompted Dabo to pump his fist in the air.

For Dabo, this was a special touchdown. J.C. Chalk, a senior tight end, was the grandson of Gene Stallings, Dabo's former coach at Alabama. It was Stallings who ultimately awarded Dabo a scholarship after he walked on to the team, and it was Stallings who offered Dabo his first job in coaching as an assistant in the Crimson Tide weight room in 1993. Dabo first met J.C. at a reunion of the '92 Alabama national championship team when J.C. was in third grade, and soon after J.C. became like family to Dabo—the Alabama connections run deep at Clemson and, in many ways, form the core of the Tiger program. After J.C. scored against Wake Forest, Dabo smiled like a proud father.

So much had changed since Dabo had taken off down that hill twelve years earlier. Clemson had made it to five straight playoffs, the only team in the country to achieve that feat. The Tigers had won two of the previous four national titles. They'd beaten twenty-two straight ACC opponents, and Dabo had won more total games over the previous five seasons (sixty-nine) than any coach in America, including the Crimson Tide's Nick Saban (sixty-six).

During the 2020 Wake Forest game, Dabo took part in both the offensive and defensive huddles, offering his perspective to assistants and players. He was also the team's most vocal cheerleader, greeting players as they came off the field, slapping backs and high-fiving, constantly clapping and encouraging, even after a play didn't go as designed. He frequently talked to the officials and rarely stopped moving, acting like a man who realized there was never enough time to accomplish all that he needed to get done.

Clemson beat Wake Forest 37–13 and was firmly entrenched as the No. 1 team in the nation. The Tiger machine was humming on all cylinders. An hour after the game, as the team buses pulled out of the parking lot and rolled into the warm Southern night, one question loomed larger than all others:

How did Dabo, in only a dozen years, build this empire?

CHAPTER 2

A HARD LIFE IN PELHAM

The young boy sat spellbound every Sunday afternoon, his face pressed close to the glow of the television in the living room, intently studying the leathery, legendary old man on the screen. *The Bear Bryant Show* was mandatory viewing on Sundays after church in the Swinneys' two-story home—white with blue shutters—at 1000 Ryecroft Circle, a corner lot in Pelham, Alabama, a growing suburb south of Birmingham. For the family and the majority of other Alabama fans in that God-fearing state, the Sunday show was an extension of the hours for worship.

Munching Golden Flake potato chips and sipping Coca-Colas—the show's two main sponsors—eight-year-old Dabo, his older brothers Tracy and Tripp, and their father, Ervil, hung on every word that tumbled out of Paul "Bear" Bryant's mouth in his gravelly, pack-a-day voice as he reviewed the flickering game film of the previous day's matchup.

Sometimes the Bear would forget a player's name or his drawl would be so thick—or, on occasion, lubricated by a few nips of Jack Daniel's—that no one could understand him, but none of that mattered to the true believers of Crimson Tide. To them, Bryant was their football god.

The game of football fired Dabo's imagination like nothing else—the Xs and Os were an intriguing chess match, the violent hitting was a sight to behold, and a well-executed offense play was a thing of pure beauty. These Sunday afternoons were some of the happiest, most carefree days of Dabo's childhood, sitting close to his dad and brothers in the living room, swaddled in the warmth of his family, feeling love, watching his coaching hero.

"People across the state would come home from church and watch the show in the afternoon," said Bill Battle, an end on Bryant's teams from 1960 to 1962 and the athletic director at Alabama from 2013 to 2017. "Bryant was so folksy that he really connected to the entire state. Sometimes you couldn't really understand him because he would mumble in that low voice of his, but that didn't matter. It was almost like church continued for the state once the show came on. His influence on kids was enormous. Not just on those who wanted to play for him, but those who would one day coach. Future coaches all across Alabama realized watching that show and saw that the best way to connect to people was to be real, authentic, charming and folksy."

Dabo proudly wore an Alabama hat as he strolled through the halls of his elementary school, sometimes even donning one of those big foam Crimson Tide hands with a raised index finger, signaling that Alabama was No. 1. He believed that one day he would put on the pads and play for Bryant in front of thousands of cheering Crimson Tide fans. And he told anyone who would listen that Alabama surely had the smartest players in America, because the school had four *A*s and one *B* in its name. There was nothing about the Crimson Tide that Dabo didn't admire. If you disagreed with him, well, you had better be ready for an argument—or even for a fist to be raised.

Dabo, his brothers, and his dad often listened to Alabama games on the radio, the play-by-play crackling out of the speaker, the voices of announcers John Forney and Doug Layton echoing across the room. The Swinneys didn't have season tickets, but the Swinney boys could close their eyes and imagine they were in the stands, fixated by the action unspooling on the football field in their minds. They never missed listening to a game, a sacred ritual in the Swinney household.

On New Year's Day, 1980, Ervil took his family to New Orleans for the Sugar Bowl, where Alabama was playing Arkansas. A family friend invited the Swinneys to the Big Easy for the game and Ervil—a Bama fan to the marrow of his bones—happily accepted the invitation, putting his boys in his car for the five-hour drive. The Swinneys visited Bourbon Street before the game, and eleven-year-old Dabo became so enthralled with a tap dancer on a street corner that he started moving and grooving with him. "My mom gave me a picture...of me tap dancing with a street guy who was a tap dancer collecting money," Dabo said. "All of these people gathered around. I was decked out in all of my Alabama stuff."

During the game, Dabo, sitting high in the rafters of the Superdome, was captivated by the play of Alabama and by the strength of Tide's running game, the power of its defense, and the coaching acumen of Bryant. The Swinneys couldn't afford to go to many Alabama games, so this was a special moment, especially for Dabo, who became more determined than ever to eventually, someday, play for the Bear.

From his Superdome seat, Dabo watched Tide running back Major Olive score two touchdowns as Alabama defeated Arkansas 24–9 to win its third national title of the decade—and the sixth and final national championship of Bryant's career. Young Dabo, outfitted in crimson-colored Alabama apparel, was overjoyed as he watched the Crimson Tide players carry their coach from the field.

It wasn't just that Bryant won games and national titles that made him so beloved throughout Dixie; it was also *how* he treated others—a characteristic that was spoken about with pride and reverence in households across the state. Bryant knew everybody's name in the football facility in Tuscaloosa—from the janitors to the cafeteria workers to the secretaries—and he was aware of their backstories. If a coach's secretary was having a bad day, for instance, Bryant would detect it and stop at her desk to offer a few encouraging words, suddenly brightening her afternoon.

"It was magic the way Coach Bryant dealt with people,

even at the end of his career," said Bruce Arians, who was the running back coach under Bryant at Alabama in 1981 and 1982, the Bear's final two seasons on the sideline. Arians, now the head coach of the Super Bowl LV champion Tampa Bay Buccaneers, added, "Coach Bryant could read others better than anyone. The importance of connecting with everyone in the program was one of the first valuable lessons I learned from him—and I think a lot of other people did too, even young people."

On January 26, 1983, a little more than three years after Bryant had won in his final national championship at the New Orleans Superdome, Dabo was walking down the hall of his middle school when he heard that Bryant had died of a heart attack at age sixty-nine. The news devastated Dabo; it was as if he'd just lost a dear family member. He had never met Bryant, but young Dabo had been positive it would only be a matter of time before Bryant would show up at a future high school game of his, watch him play, and offer him a scholarship. But now that fantasy had been crushed.

Two days later, the entire state of Alabama came to a virtual standstill as Bryant's hearse rolled west on Interstate 20/59. All along the fifty-five-mile route from the First United Methodist Church in Tuscaloosa to Elmwood Cemetery in Birmingham, thousands of fans had stopped their cars and pickup trucks and eighteen-wheelers to watch the procession of three hundred vehicles motor by, their headlights aglow in the gray winter afternoon. Standing on overpasses, business-men placed fedoras over their hearts, farmers in overalls put hands on their chests, and children in Crimson Tide jackets had tears rolling down their cheeks. Everyone's face looked frozen as they said their final good-bye to the Bear, who left this world the winningest coach in college football history.

Bruce Arians attended the funeral. He had spoken to Bryant only a few weeks before the Bear died, telling him in his office that he had accepted the head coaching position at Temple University. Arians asked him questions about recruiting and organization, and then Bryant told him about the nature of coaching—and life, really. The words he uttered may as well have been spoken to little Dabo, because they underscored Bryant's core coaching philosophy—an outlook that would one day serve as the bedrock of Dabo's own.

"Coach them hard and hug them harder later," Bryant told Arians. "Find out what makes a player tick and continually build on the player's strengths and not prey on their weaknesses. You always need to fix some of their weaknesses, but you first pad their confidence so that that it grows and then they can attack their weaknesses. Be hard on your players when we're on the field. But that's just coaching. The players need to know that you're probably going to talk to them real ugly out on the field, but that has nothing to do with them personally or with their personality. They can struggle with football and still be good kids. They need to know they can't take it personally. It's coaching, not a criticism.

"When you walk off the field, tell them that you're going to get their football right, that we're not going to beat ourselves," Bryant continued in his final conversation with Arians. "And once you're done with football for the day, you can talk all night long with your players about their personal lives. You need to care about all of your players, from the starting quarterback down to the third string tight end. That's the prime role of a college head coach. You must help [your] players grow into young men of substance—men with confidence, character, and knowledge beyond the field. That's what makes coaching football so special. You can have a real impact on these kids' lives. And remember to make sure that [they] write letters to their mammas. It's important to let the mammas know that you are taking care of their boy."

For days, Dabo mourned the loss of his coach. But for a lifetime, the influence of Paul "Bear" Bryant—and especially his belief that you *coach them hard and hug them harder*— would impact Dabo.

FROM THE START, HE looked ready to rumble. On November 20, 1969, Carol Swinney gave birth to son number three at South Highlands Hospital in Birmingham, husband Ervil by her side. As soon as he was placed in Carol's arms for the first time, the newborn thrust both fists into the air, as if fixin' for a tussle. Carol immediately said, "Uh oh, he's going to be a fighter."

Carol planned to call the child Chris. But Tripp, her eighteen-month-old son, had difficulty enunciating the name. In his toddler Southern drawl, he insisted on calling him "That Boy." But when those two words were formed in his mouth, they came out in his little kid Alabama twang sounding like "Dabo."

The name stuck. Dabo wouldn't know until he was in third grade that his given name—the one that appeared on his birth certificate—was William Christopher Swinney.

In the beginning, Ervil was a loving, caring family man. He had married Carol McGraw two weeks after she graduated from Woodlawn High in 1962. He eventually owned a pair of washer and dryer repair service stores, where he regaled customers with stories and his lightning-quick wit. In 1969, he moved his wife and three children into a two-story home on Ryecroft Circle in Pelham. The house was a magnet to neighborhood kids, who would come over and play games with the Swinney boys—basketball in the street and football and baseball in the backyard. Carol, a stay-at-home mom who volunteered at her kids' various schools, served drinks and treats such as double-chocolate muffins in the screened-in back porch when there was a break in the action. When Ervil wasn't working, he coached his boys in Little League, threw the ball with them in the yard, and was as present in their daily routines as he could be. At Christmas he hung outdoor lights and put plastic snowmen and reindeer in the front yard. On Christmas Eve, with the three Swinney boys tucked under the covers in the same bed, Ervil climbed onto the roof, his footfalls sounding like Santa had arrived. For the first years of Dabo's life, his childhood was reminiscent of a Norman Rockwell print—the idyllic nuclear family, Southern-style.

School and sports came easy to young Dabo. In grade school, he flashed an agile mind, able to memorize information and then verbalize what he had just learned with startling accuracy. A curious boy, he longed for knowledge. He sometimes repeated his homework assignments if he felt like he didn't fully understand what he had just studied. Everything had to be done the right way, even if it meant spending extra hours with his nose buried in his books. His teachers adored his work ethic, noting his rare commitment to learning.

His classmates were drawn to him; during recess he always seemed to be at the hub of activity, the center of a crowd. He inherited his father's sense of humor, and Dabo liked to tell jokes and entertain his classmates. He never lacked for friends. When teams were picked for various playground games, he was often the first kid selected, because, even as early as grade school, he excelled in football, basketball, and baseball. The best part of athletics, to young Dabo, was the camaraderie of being on a team, of being a part of something that was bigger than him.

Dabo tagged along with his older brother Tracy to his baseball practices. He couldn't get enough of sports; they were the air he breathed, the sun in his solar system. Later, when Tracy attended Marion Military Institute—a military junior college in Marion, Alabama—Dabo would often travel with his mom sixty-five miles south of Pelham to see his games. Dabo liked to arrive early and hang out in the clubhouse, watching the players interact. He saw how the game of baseball had bonded them all together. He noticed how—regardless of their disparate backgrounds—they seemed to genuinely care for one another, which deepened Dabo's infatuation with clubhouses and locker rooms. Dabo became such a presence at Marion

Military Institute that he was virtually a member of its base-ball team, shagging balls in the outfield before games and encouraging the players like he was their batboy and number one fan.

By practicing and mimicking his brothers, Dabo quickly blossomed into a talented baseball player, beginning at the Little League level. At age ten he'd step to the plate and pivot his stance so it looked like he was about to hit the ball toward third base. This would cause the coaches on the opposing team to shift their players on the field, expecting Dabo to hit where he was aiming. But then, just before he'd swing, Dabo would adjust his feet at the last moment, seeing a gaping hole in the middle of the field. He'd then blast the ball into the open space over second base. Even at a young age, Dabo could figure out how to beat a defense that was designed to stop him.

Before an all-star game, the public address announcer leaned into the microphone and gave the starting lineups. When he said, "William Swinney," Dabo didn't budge. But a few heartbeats later, he realized the announcer was referring to him. "Oh, that's me, isn't it?" he said. William Swinney dashed out onto the field and lined up along the baseline with his teammates, shaking his head that he hadn't even recognized the name his parents had given him at birth.

ONE DAY IN 1984, Tripp Swinney—Dabo's older brother—was riding in the front passenger seat of a friend's car. One block from the Swinney house, the driver lost control of the vehicle and crashed into a neighbor's house. The impact was so violent that Tripp, sixteen, was catapulted through the windshield. By the time paramedics arrived, Tripp was clinging to life. He suffered severe head trauma. As the EMTs rushed him to the hospital, they feared he wouldn't survive.

Doctors told Carol the knee-buckling news that her son was in bad shape, that he might not make it. For several weeks, Tripp's eyes remained shut as he lay in a coma. Carol stayed by his bedside as much as she could, praying that her son would regain consciousness. He eventually did, but he didn't recognize anyone—not his mom, not Dabo, not any family members.

Carol showed Tripp one photo after the next, hoping it would trigger a memory. But the accident had wiped all of his experiences from his mind, as if the reel of film from his life had been erased the moment he flew through that windshield. Then one day, out of the blue and after Tripp had been released from the hospital and was at home, the family dog barked. The poodle kept barking.

"Shut up, Peppy!" Tripp yelled.

In an instant, Tripp's memory returned—the film of his past life started to play out in vivid, beautiful colors. He eventually recognized his mom, his dad, his brothers, his friends, and his dog. His mind was healing.

A tragedy had been averted. But in the Swinney household, more storm clouds gathered on the horizon.

THE FRACTURING OF THE family began in the mid-1980s when Ervil's washing machine repair shops started to lose money. His family had grown accustomed to living a middle-class lifestyle, complete with the nice house and decent cars, and rarely hesitating to purchase something if it was really needed. Ervil desperately wanted to keep taking care of his family the way he always had, covering the mortgage and all the other expenses with his paychecks from his service business. But as his debts mounted and he sank deeper and deeper into financial distress, Ervil hid his money problems from his family, too proud to tell them what was happening. He didn't ask anyone for help or guidance. Instead, he began to withdraw from his normal social circle and found solace in the bottle.

He could be a mean drunk, according to family friends, the opposite of his joking, happy-go-lucky self when he was sober. He started going to bars, drowning his sorrows and nights away—meeting his personal demon. He'd come home in the small hours of the morning and sometimes start yelling, unleashing all the pent-up emotion inside of him, taking out all of his frustration on his family. When Carol would confront him about what was happening and tell him that he needed to go to bed and sleep it off, the boys sometimes had to restrain Ervil, keeping him from getting to their mom.

His drinking grew more severe—and so did his financial woes. By this time, Tracy was at college and Tripp had left to attend the University of Montevallo, meaning Dabo—who sometimes didn't have any lunch money in his pocket when he went to school—was the only son still living on Ryecroft Circle. Many times Ervil didn't come home, disappearing for days. Carol and Dabo would drive around looking for him, hoping they wouldn't discover the worst. And when Ervil did return home, the yelling and screaming would commence again. Scared, young Dabo would crawl through a window to sit on the roof, crying as he looked at the stars, trying to make sense of it all, trying to figure out a way to make his dad stop. He loved his father dearly—that would never change—but he couldn't understand why he drank so much alcohol. It changed his dad as a person. But the next morning, after Ervil had sobered up, he was the loving, caring, doting father again.

Ervil didn't get the help he needed, and kept failing and falling toward his rock bottom. Drunk and enraged after coming home from his local watering hole, he'd punch walls, throw lamps, and break windows. Police were called more than once, including one particular December night when he tossed the Christmas tree across the living room.

On many nights, Carol would put Dabo in the car and they'd head to a hotel to escape Ervil's wrath. Dabo never stopped loving his dad, but he was humiliated by his father's actions. How could he not be? The neighbors knew what was happening inside their house, and it was getting harder and harder to keep his secret from his friends. Some of the roughest, most restless nights were when Carol and Dabo slept in their car that was parked deep in the woods, too afraid to go home.

Ready or not, Dabo the boy had to grow up.

HE NEEDED TO MAKE some money. So starting at age fourteen, he got into the business of cleaning gutters. Dabo, along with his friend Les Daniels, would go to the nearby upper-class neighborhood of Riverchase and start knocking on doors. Carrying a ladder, a blower, and a rake, Dabo and Les would ask strangers if they'd like to have the leaves removed from their gutters—for a fee, of course.

Even at this young age, Dabo had a way with words. According to former customers, Dabo would promise to perform the most thorough cleaning job of anyone alive. If it took several hours to extract those leaves and whatever other muck resided in their gutters, Dabo swore that he and his buddy wouldn't stop until the job was done to perfection, that the gutters would be so clean that a raging river of rain could fall from the sky and those gutters would handle every drop of the deluge.

Dabo was also smart about picking his customers. He targeted the biggest homes, because those jobs took the longest and paid the best. Not surprisingly, the talkative, pleasant-looking young Dabo developed a friendship with many of his paying customers, speaking to them about their own families, the sports he played, and—naturally—all things Crimson Tide football. Dabo and his buddy became such a presence in the neighborhood that their customers started expecting them to come, refusing the business of other industrious young men because they believed so much in this kid Dabo Swinney.

None of them knew, of course, of the personal hell he was living through in his own home.

OVER THE SPAN OF a few years, Ervil's debt continued to grow. It eventually reached a quarter million dollars. By the time

Dabo was a sophomore in high school, his father could no longer afford the $60 mortgage payment on their home on Ryecroft Circle. The bank foreclosed on the house—the place the family had called home for a decade.

At age sixteen, Dabo—hurt and confused—and his mother moved into a small townhome. Unable to afford movers, Dabo asked a handful of his coaches and friends to help them haul their suitcases, packed boxes, and furnishings to their new address, amplifying his embarrassment. The secret of his dad's shortcomings was now out in the open. Children of alcoholics often will go to great lengths to conceal what is really happening in their homes, and Dabo was no different. But now virtually all of the important people in young Dabo's life knew the pain he was enduring. His father moved into a trailer behind one of his businesses. Dabo placed many of his own belongings in a storage shed.

Carol had been a stay-at-home mom, but now she had to earn a paycheck. She landed a job at a Birmingham department store, earning $8 an hour standing behind a counter. But the money she brought in wasn't enough to cover the rent. After a few months, Carol and her son came home to an eviction notice that had been posted on the door. For a time Carol stayed at her mom's house while Dabo bounced around from one friend's family to the next, sleeping on couches or wherever he could find space.

Wanting to be together, they eventually both moved into the home of one of Dabo's high school friends. Carol stayed upstairs in a room close to the mother and sister while Dabo crashed downstairs. Each night he'd pull an egg-crate-like mattress from under a couch and then lay down on the floor; in the morning he'd cram it back under the couch. During one stretch of time, Dabo lived with his grandmother in a government-subsidized apartment that was about the size of his family's old living room on Ryecroft Circle.

When Dabo was in eleventh grade, his older brother Tracy told their mother that it was time for her to leave their father, time to bury the pain and the past and move forward. Carol eventually agreed, and Dabo's parents divorced his junior year at Pelham High School. Needing to be alone to process what he had just heard, Dabo walked into the school's athletic field house and cried. He felt like his life, already in tatters, had officially fallen apart, like he was in the middle of a storm that he couldn't escape. His older brothers were away at school, so he couldn't lean on them for support. He was alone, never more so than when he was in that field house, the tears falling down his young cheeks.

But despite the emotional pain that he was in, and as confused as he was, Dabo still earned good enough grades to make the honor roll and he never stopped excelling at sports— football, basketball, and baseball. He was immensely focused, and in many ways sports became his escape, the place where he could hit pause on his problems and lose himself in the joy and wonder and thrill of competition. According to friends, he never allowed himself to wallow in self-pity, to wonder why his lot in life had been so challenging, to let his frustrations subsume him or derail the dreams he had for his own future— namely, to attend the University of Alabama. Still, when he played varsity football at Pelham, the cheerleaders placed signs and notes on the front doors of the players' homes. But with Dabo, they didn't know where his front door was.

"Dabo had this tight circle of friends who all came from really good, strong families," said Matt Coulter, a Swinney family friend who has been a longtime television and radio personality in Birmingham. "Virtually all of his friends had fathers who became positive influences on Dabo. I really think that helped save him. He had had so many people who loved him and supported him and were always asking how he was doing. We played a lot of basketball together in those days—man, he had a pretty-looking jump shot—and he was hyper-competitive but always fair. Sports were his escape, no question, but it was his friends, their fathers and his mother who really got him through some of the toughest times in his life."

Dabo even tried to support and comfort his mom, telling her constantly that a new dawn was coming, that better days for them were ahead, that together they would make it through the tough times and one day look back at them as a period of growth and development. "Mama, don't worry," Dabo would say. "We'll be okay. It's gonna work out."

Whenever Dabo said something like that, Carol shook her head in astonishment. She always knew her youngest son was special, but now she truly understood that there was just something *different* about dat boy Dabo.

DABO INHERITED HIS TOUGHNESS and resolve and never-quit attitude from his mother. Dabo knew the story of her childhood well. Whenever he had an inclination to feel down and out about something, to slip into a pit of woe-is-me despair, he'd think about all that his mom achieved—even though she had been told repeatedly in her youth that she'd never walk again.

Carol McGraw was born in Clanton, Alabama, located near the geographic center of the state and home of the Chilton County Peach Festival since 1947. The youngest of four children, Carol was a healthy ten-pound baby. But before she celebrated her second birthday, she contracted polio, which during the 1940s killed or paralyzed more than five hundred thousand people around the world each year. The disease hit Carol hard: She suffered paralysis and high fevers. Her parents sent her to a hospital in Birmingham, where she was put in isolation and an iron lung helped her breathe. Her muscles weakened, but once she was well enough, she moved to what was called Birmingham Crippled Children's Hospital for a long, difficult, painful rehabilitation.

Her physical nightmare was only beginning. At age six, while still in the hospital, doctors discovered that Carol had a severe case of scoliosis, her spine wickedly curved by the polio. To try to straighten her spine, doctors wrapped her in a head-to-knees cast for about a year. She then spent another year in a cast that was slightly smaller and underwent two spinal fusions. Once she had recovered from the surgeries and the casts had been cut off, doctors placed a large metal brace around her torso and back, which she couldn't remove for another year. When she finally shed the brace, she was pushed around the hospital in a wheelchair and told she would likely never lead a normal life and possibly never walk. But she never gave up, constantly fantasizing of having her own family and her own home in a quiet neighborhood with manicured lawns and kids riding through the streets on their bicycles. The dream sustained her.

Carol spent a total of eleven years in various hospitals. She didn't have any close friends and really didn't know her three siblings. Teachers taught her reading, writing, and arithmetic in the hospital as she lay in her bed; later, when she gained enough stamina, she would climb into a wheelchair to be pushed to a hospital classroom, but she was so weak that she had trouble writing on the chalkboard. Doctors feared that the extended isolation she experienced during her decade-plus stay in the hospital had carved deep psychological scars. So when she was released from the hospital just before she turned thirteen, the doctors told her to stay as active as possible—she still needed to strengthen her atrophied muscles—and be as social as possible.

After a year of being taught at home, Carol began her public school education in the ninth grade. By all accounts, she was a happy, grateful young woman, quick to smile. When friends learned of the ordeal she had been through—the years in the hospital, the decade of loneliness—they marveled at her positive outlook on life. Rather than view her past as one that was filled with darkness and desperation, she chose to focus on how lucky she was to have surmounted the obstacles that she faced, how fortunate she had been to have received such wonderful treatment from so many doctors, and now how fun it was to lead a somewhat "normal" life and have friends. Not a day went by that she felt bitter. Not a day went by that she didn't count her blessings.

Once in public school, Carol spotted another girl twirling a baton, which inspired her to sign up for a dance class. Oh, how far she had come from being so weak in the hospital that she had to prop up her right hand with her left just so she could write on the chalkboard. Now she practiced dancing and baton twirling at all hours, trying to become the best dancer in the school. And that was just what she did: She was named a lead majorette in the school marching band. It was such an arresting, fascinating story—a girl goes from spending a decade in a hospital room to becoming the young woman who led the band onto the football field on Friday nights—that the editors of the *Birmingham News* Sunday magazine sent a reporter to her school to interview her and describe how she had overcome polio. Days later, Carol's picture appeared on the cover of the magazine under the headline "Cinderella Never Had It So Good" and was accompanied by a lengthy story about her journey. She was the definition of a survivor.

Carol's fortitude would never leave her. When things were at their worst with Ervil—when she and Dabo would sleep in her car or when they would leave in the middle of night, not sure where they would go—she channeled that inner strength that was forged during her childhood. She never stopped believing in the power of possibility.

But then there were times she'd look over at young Dabo,

and he would be the one reassuring her that everything would be fine, that together they would make it through the dark and find that light again. Her son was practically inviting her to lean on him. Turned out, Dabo was a carbon copy of his momma.

HE FIRST MET THIS girl when he was in second grade. She was a year behind him at Valley Elementary School in Pelham, and he felt drawn to her, even at his age: seven. Her name was Kathleen Bassett. It didn't take long for little Dabo to develop a crush on little Kathleen.

In fourth grade, Dabo discovered that Kathleen wanted to become a member of the school's safety patrol team. Problem was, students had to be elected to be on the team. Dabo had as many friends as any kid in his class, and he told anyone who would listen to vote for Kathleen. He was the ultimate campaign manager, and Kathleen was elected to the high office of safety patrol. At the tender age of nine, she had discovered the powers of Dabo's persuasion.

Dabo's oldest brother started dating Kathleen's older sister, and Dabo and Kathleen would hang out at her house, playing, laughing, talking—just being together. They became the closest of friends. A few years later, Dabo handwrote a note and gave it to Kathleen, asking her to accompany him to a school dance. She marked the "yes" box and the date was on. They were officially "going together," as it was called back in the early 1980s.

Dabo still keeps a copy of a photo from the Riverchase

Middle School Dance in his office, the night he took his future wife out for the first time. Snapped in 1982, the yellowed photograph shows Kathleen Bassett outfitted in a blue dress with a red belt as bright as a stoplight. She's holding flowers. Dabo is adorned in a light-colored patterned jacket, white shirt, and brown necktie. In the picture his eyebrows are raised—as if he can't believe how lucky he is—and his left arm is gently wrapped around Kathleen's shoulder. They both are smiling wide.

Kathleen has a calming character and sugary, soothing Southern accent. They broke up the following year after not seeing each other for three weeks over Christmas break, with Dabo telling her at lunch, "You know, I just don't want a girlfriend right now. I just want to be great friends." Instead of being angry, Kathleen—easygoing and not easily agitated—simply said, "Oh, it's okay. It's not a problem."

They reignited their romance at Pelham High. In 1987, on their first high school date, Dabo took Kathleen to a restaurant in Hoover, another suburb of Birmingham. He had $10 in his wallet. Kathleen ordered mozzarella sticks, which Dabo had never heard of before, and water, not wanting to overtop Dabo's modest means. They then went to see the movie *Summer School*, where actor Mark Harmon plays a gym teacher who is forced to teach a remedial English class during the summer. But the movie, which flopped at the box office, didn't start until 9:45 p.m. At about 10:45, Kathleen told her date that she needed to be home—which was a twenty-five-minute drive away—by 11:00. They ran to Dabo's car and he lead-footed it back to Pelham. Alas, she missed her curfew and was grounded the next weekend. But that didn't extinguish their blooming love. For the rest of their time at Pelham High, they were the yearbook-perfect pair—Dabo was the big-time sports star; Kathleen the oh-so-pretty cheerleader. Some of their friends remarked that they had never seen a cuter, happier, more striking young couple.

At first, Dabo attempted to conceal his family problems from Kathleen. She came from a normal, educated, stable family, and he worried that she would run away at high speed from him if he shared what was happening in his own home. But then he finally opened up to her. She listened to her boyfriend as he described the horrors of his childhood, his dad's problems, and his family's downward spiral. Kathleen supported him, telling him how much she admired him, making sure he stayed focused on school and the people who loved him. With Kathleen by his side, Dabo didn't have the time—or the inclination—to dwell on anything negative. They talked through everything.

And that, really, was how Dabo would deal with everything for the rest of his life: He would discuss it, especially with Kathleen and his mom. He would break down a problem, analyze it from every angle, and figure out a solution, rarely hiding how he truly felt. Always, Dabo moved forward, no matter how menacing or massive the problem in front of him.

ON FEBRUARY 3, 1986, Dabo and a friend drove to Pelham High for a Fellowship of Christian Athletes event. Dabo was close with Stewart Wiley, a youth football coach who started the FCA group at Pelham High, and Wiley encouraged Dabo to get involved with the organization. Dabo, then sixteen, wanted to attend this particular meeting in 1986 because the featured speaker was Joey Jones, a star receiver for Alabama and one of Dabo's all-time favorite college football players.

Dabo expected Jones to tell stories about the football team in Tuscaloosa. Instead, he talked about how he had accepted God into his life and how that had changed everything for him. Dabo was so moved by Jones's words—and by the spirit—that he wound up praying with Jones after the talk and accepting Christ as his Lord and Savior. After the meeting was over, Dabo went home, walked into his bedroom, and wrote down the date in his Bible: "February 3, 1986—I dedicated my life to the Lord today, and He will be with me forever."

Dabo was born again. Starting that evening, his faith would not only be at the center of his life—indeed be the very core of it—but it would also be the foundation of his coaching. It would always bring him comfort, be his North Star—but it would also one day bring on professional controversy.

HIS HIGH SCHOOL FOOTBALL career was successful. A three-year starter for Pelham High's coach Billy Tohill, Dabo was named a *Birmingham News* Scholar-Athlete winner. He was a capable receiver—former teammates have remarked over the years about his good hands and his solid blocking—but he lacked top speed and, at 6'1" and 165 pounds, was thin. The coaching staff adored him: He never had to be told something twice and he ran his passing routes with textbook precision. If he had just been a little bigger and a little faster, perhaps he could have attracted the attention of Division I football recruiters, but his physical limitations made his dream of earning a scholarship to Alabama or any other Southeastern Conference school far-fetched at best. A realist, Dabo admitted this to his close friends.

Still, he possessed terrific hand-eye coordination, which he displayed on the basketball court. As a senior at Pelham, he earned all-metro honors as a wing player on the Pelham High basketball team. He also flourished at golf and tennis—two of his favorite hobbies. Sports had always been an outlet of sorts for Dabo, and if he wasn't studying or hanging out with Kathleen during high school, he was typically playing something.

Dabo was a senior when he coached his first football game. With a whistle draped around his neck, he played the role of Pelham head football coach Bill Tohill in the junior-senior powder-puff football game. Little did anyone know this afternoon on the football field would turn out to be a showcase event of what was to come.

Man, he was into that game, directing his young female players here and there, drawing up plays in the dirt, teaching the fundamentals of blocking. A few of Dabo's friends stepped back and noticed that he was in his element; he looked like a coaching natural. Dabo had planned to attend his dream school, the University of Alabama, as a regular student—no football scholarship was ever offered—and maybe, one friend thought after watching him on this day, he could be a student manager for the Crimson Tide.

No one remembers if Dabo's team won that afternoon, but the images of him on the sideline—encouraging, high-fiving, smiling, uplifting, having the time of his life—still remains vivid to the few who were there on the day that Dat Boy coached his first football game.

CHAPTER 3

DEFYING THE ODDS IN TUSCALOOSA

They sat close together in the student section of Alabama's Bryant–Denny Stadium, this boy and his girl, outfitted in Crimson-colored clothes, holding hands and cheering their beloved Crimson Tide. Dabo, a freshman at the school, attended on Pell Grants and student loans, and despite his adoration of all things Alabama, he had no intention of playing college football. He planned to major in premed biology and hoped to one day became a pediatrician. One of his heroes growing up was Dr. Edward Goldblatt, the only doctor who ever treated Dabo, dating to the day he came into the world in the autumn of 1969.

Dabo enjoyed science. It came easy to him; formulas and numbers, rules and methods were a familiar universe, and throughout high school he consistently made good grades in science and math classes. Now in the early days of college, he wanted to dedicate his life to helping others, which meant years of undergraduate and graduate school—and years of mounting student debt. But then something happened on this Saturday afternoon at Bryant–Denny. Surrounded by students adorned in houndstooth attire with crimson-and-white shakers in their hands and constantly yelling "Roll Tide!" Dabo was suddenly struck with an overwhelming thought, as if the Bear himself had thrown a lightning bolt at him from above to trigger this realization: He missed football—dearly. He missed not just the games, but also the locker room, the joking with his teammates, the discipline of memorizing the playbook, the team meetings, the long practices, the rush of adrenaline of making a bone-jarring block, the thrill of possibility every time he stepped between the white lines, and the togetherness of just being one of the guys.

He understood that he was a skinny, slow-footed wide receiver who, on paper, probably had no business playing in the Southeastern Conference. But he knew he had certain strengths and attributes that could help a team like Alabama—drive, heart, an internal motor that never stopped revving, and a willingness to do whatever it took to make himself and his teammates better. He was a classic overachiever—his high school coaches marveled at how he squeezed every ounce of his potential into on-the-field production—and as he watched this third Alabama game of the season with Kathleen, he believed he could contribute to the Tide. After seeing a few wide receivers drop some easy down-the-field catches, he turned to Kathleen, a senior at Pelham High at the time, and said, "I can do that. I know I'm good enough to play."

Believing in himself—one of the hallmarks of Dabo's character—he set up a meeting with Rich Wingo, the Alabama strength coach who was also the walk-on coordinator. Raising his chin high and staring into the eyes of the coach, Dabo declared that he wanted to walk on to the Crimson Tide football team. He explained that he couldn't let the game go, he just couldn't. The sport had cast a powerful, alluring spell over him years before—the most magical moments of his childhood had been watching *The Bear Bryant Show* with his father in the family living room—and now he told Wingo that he could make the Alabama team as a walk-on for one reason: No one would outwork, out-hustle, or out-study him.

Wingo was skeptical. This fresh-faced Swinney kid sure didn't look like he could play in the SEC, or even at the junior college level for that matter. But the coach told Dabo that he would give him a chance the following spring, explaining that he could show up at tryouts with forty-six other dreamers who wanted to walk on to the Tide. Dabo left the meeting smiling like a student who had just aced a critical exam.

He immediately went to work, spending hours in the weight room, desperately trying to gain muscle mass and weight. He'd rise around 5:00 a.m. three times a week and, usually alone, would walk through the early-morning darkness to the sprawling Alabama weight room. Several players remember Dabo typically lifting like he was in a hurry, as if each session and each rep was more vital than the last.

Yet what the players *couldn't* see about Dabo was more important than what they could: specifically, how his childhood had toughened him. Through all the struggles he had endured due to the dysfunction and decay of his family, Dabo never allowed himself to drown in a pool of self-pity, to curse at his lot in life. Because of his experiences, he thoroughly believed that there were no obstacles he couldn't leap over. In Dabo's world, there were only opportunities. What really mattered was what you *did* with those opportunities. Advance, never retreat—this was Dabo's philosophy in life and in sports.

RICH WINGO DIDN'T KNOW Dabo's name, but he knew one thing about the small kid from Pelham: He was tough— country tough. And he always seemed to be smiling, like he had stepped into a dream. "He didn't have all the confidence in the world like he does now, but he was still a confident young man, especially given the fact that he was such a long shot to make the team," said Wingo. "I worked his butt off."

Forty-seven young men showed up for the first day of tryouts, which took place three days a week in January and February in the practice gym on the lower level of the Coleman Coliseum basketball arena. It didn't take long for the torture tests to commence. Before one running drill, Wingo turned up the thermostat into the triple digits, transforming the training area in Coleman into a sauna. Then the strength coach ordered his players to run sprint after sprint after sprint. Garbage cans were placed around the arena, and soon players were seen bent over and losing whatever food and fluid they had put into their mouths that morning.

Dabo kept coming back for more pain, still believing that

he could beat the odds and be one of the two or three players who could earn a chance to participate in spring practice in March. After the walk-on workouts were over, the announcement was made: Dabo was one of two who would be allowed to suit up with the team in the spring. He later called himself a "crawl-on," because of the harsh, knee-buckling, survival-of-the-fittest nature of the tryouts.

Dabo got in for a few plays in the spring game in April—he hustled on every snap like every coach was judging him, even if the ball didn't come his way—and that summer he practiced with the varsity. He was still a walk-on, still buried so low on the depth chart at wide receiver that he knew he could be let go at any time, but he was inching closer to his boyhood fantasy of dressing for the Tide on a game day. What made his life even sweeter was that Kathleen, his girlfriend, had enrolled at Alabama that fall. Their long-distance romance was now a close-campus commute—and would be for the rest of their lives.

Before the fall semester of his redshirt freshman year began—late August 1989—Dabo walked to Coleman one afternoon to register for classes. But then an administrator told him there was a problem: There was an issue with his Pell Grant application. The administrator said the paperwork for the grant had not gone through, which meant he wouldn't be eligible to receive the money. Dabo was confused and devastated; without the Pell Grant, he wouldn't be able to pay for his tuition.

In a panic, Dabo said that his family's finances were a mess because of his father's erratic, irresponsible behavior. But the administrator was unmoved. It was explained to Dabo that if he couldn't pay the school the base tuition of $580, which was half the tuition expense for one semester, he wouldn't be allowed to sign up for classes. What was more, Dabo was behind on his rent; he owed his landlord $400. At this moment, Dabo thought his days at Alabama could be numbered and that his football career would have to be put on hold.

Crestfallen, Dabo headed back to his apartment. Once inside, he picked up the phone and, crying, called his mom, telling her that because of the financial disarray his dad had put them in that he was going to have to come home to Pelham. For several minutes, the tears streamed down the cheeks of both Dabo and his mom. At one point Dabo dropped to his knees, praying to God for help, for guidance, for some type of miracle that could keep him in Tuscaloosa. In this emotional moment, Dabo believed he'd have to drop out of school at Alabama. He'd take some junior college classes somewhere, save money, and not play football. If he ever did reenroll at Alabama, he was fully aware that, as a walk-on, he'd be long shot to remake the team, because walk-ons aren't typically afforded second chances.

Dabo was heartbroken. But in his world, no matter how much pain you are in, you always take one step forward, then another, then another, searching for that next opportunity. And so he did. Minutes after hanging up with his mom, he checked his mailbox. He grabbed a stack of letters and flyers and placed them on the coffee table in his apartment. He spotted an envelope with a Discover card logo emblazoned on it. This didn't make sense: He didn't have a Discover card. He opened the envelope, finding two blank checks and a letter explaining he was a Discover card member and he was eligible to withdraw money immediately.

Dabo was confused. He didn't recall ever signing up for the card. He dialed 1-800-DISCOVER. A customer service representative answered, and Dabo peppered her with questions. She calmly informed him that he was, in fact, a new cardholder and that as a new cardholder he had access to checks. Dabo said to the rep that he didn't have a card. She put him on hold; she needed to check with her supervisor on what she should do.

Was this a mistake? Was this the answer to his prayers? Dabo didn't know what to think, but he realized that his ability to stay at Alabama was now in the hands of a customer representative located in some faraway office. One minute passed, then two.

After a few tense minutes—his immediate football future hanging in the balance—the woman came back on the line and explained that the card had been mailed to him months earlier but that it had gone to the wrong address and was returned. Dabo never saw it. "If you give me your address, we'll send you another one," she said. "In the meantime, you can use those checks to draw on your account."

"Wait a minute!" Dabo said. "You mean I've got a Discover card?"

"Yeah, because of your grades," she said. "It's a student program, and you've qualified for it."

"You're telling me I can take these right now and use them like it's a checking account?" he asked.

"Yes," she said. "Up to your credit limit."

"What's my credit limit?" he asked.

"A thousand dollars," she replied.

Dabo yelled in joy and started to cry. He called his mom back, some twenty minutes after their last conversation, and told her that the Lord had just granted him a miracle, had answered a prayer. He strolled back to Coleman, feeling like God was guiding his every step, and promptly wrote a check to the school registrar. He then went and rapped on the door of his landlord, handing him a check for $400. Dabo was now about $1,000 in debt, but at least he could stay at Alabama—and stay on the football team. And Dabo already believed, at age nineteen, he had made the best investment he could: betting on himself.

THE FORGING OF DABO'S character began years earlier on those scary, sleepless nights when he would wait for his dad to come home from the bar, wondering if violence would erupt. He had seen a lot in his young life—things that were so much more important than Xs and Os or making a football team—and he had learned how to deal with hardships. In many ways life hadn't been fair to Dabo, but now he believed all of his past experiences had prepared him to make a positive impact on the Alabama football team, even if it was only to be a fourth-team scout player who went against first-team defensive backs in practice.

But like any college student, Dabo wasn't perfect. At the start of his redshirt freshman season, he hadn't yet made the varsity traveling roster. Instead of hitting the road with their teammates on Fridays, these players participated in a 5:30 a.m. scrimmage in full pads on the AstroTurf practice field. The players detested it—"They would put us in jail if we tried to do something like that now," Swinney said—but the nontraveling players also knew that if they wanted to climb the depth chart, they needed to show up and put forth maximum effort, playing with full-throttled intensity.

One Friday that fall, Dabo's alarm failed to go off. He woke up at 7:00 a.m.—ninety minutes after the scrimmage had started. He descended into a category-five panic, wondering what he should do. If he ran over to the practice field, the coaches would see that he was late and the punishment would be swift, severe, and—quite possibly—cruel and unusual. There were about one hundred fifteen players at the time who weren't on the traveling roster, and every single one of them except Dabo was at the scrimmage. Dabo came up with an idea: He wouldn't go. *They won't miss me,* he thought. *I'm a nobody. They won't care.*

Dabo skipped the scrimmage. On Monday he attended practice just like he always did, figuring he had gotten away with his absence and had pulled a fast one on his coaches. Monday was a light, easy practice day—the traveling players were still physically recovering from the game on Saturday—and not a single coach said anything to Dabo. Leaving the practice field on Monday, Dabo was sure that he was in the clear.

Tuesday the team dressed in full pads. Dabo was in what football players and coaches call "flex" and stretching when strength coach Rich Wingo—who was still in charge of the walk-ons—approached. "Mr. Swinney," Wingo said, "you will be with me when flex is over."

"Yes, sir," Dabo replied.

Practice began, but for Dabo it was a marathon running and sprinting session. "I am going to try to run you off today," Wingo told Dabo. In full pads and in view of his teammates, Dabo never stopped moving for over an hour. Wingo—a former Green Bay Packers linebacker who was now half strength coach and half drill sergeant—stood nearby, yelling for Dabo to keep moving his legs, to keep pushing forward. He was teaching his young player a lesson about being on time—for the rest of his career as a player and a coach, Dabo would be early for virtually every meeting—but Wingo also wanted to see what kind of toughness this kid possessed.

Specifically, Wingo was testing Dabo, trying to gauge whether or not he was fit to be the kind of gutty, gritty scout team player who would give 100 percent against the first team Alabama defense, no matter how much pain he was in. Wingo didn't say it, but he was impressed: Dabo, drenched in so much sweat it looked like he had been swimming in a pool, survived the practice, never falling, never asking for mercy, never asking for a break. Varsity and nonvarsity players alike witnessed the brutal workout that Dabo was being forced to endure, and they all knew that Coach Wingo was trying to get this young, nobody walk-on to quit the team on the spot.

But Dabo, mouth shut, just kept running and running and running.

The whistle blew to signal the end of practice, and Dabo collapsed to the ground. Several of his teammates carried him off the field and into the locker room. The next day Dabo was in so much pain—his muscles were sore in places he didn't even know he had places—he didn't go to class. But after staying in bed for most of the morning, he limped over to the football facility and forced his way back out onto the practice field.

Seeing Dabo in the flex line before practice, Wingo again approached his young redshirt walk-on. Was it possible that more hell on Earth awaited Dabo? Wingo cracked the thinnest of smiles. "Mr. Swinney, I want you to come lead us in flex today."

Dabo—a player who virtually no one on the team had ever heard of, a player no one knew a lick about—then jogged to the front of the team. As players quietly asked each other, "Who's that?" Dabo began leading the team in jumping jacks and other warm-up drills. For the first time, all eyes of Alabama football were on the kid from Pelham. From this day forward, he had won over his teammates. From this day forward, he was no longer just a walk-on. Now he was one of the guys.

AT THE START OF his redshirt freshman year, Dabo had more on his mind than just football and academics. His mom, Carol Swinney, was struggling to pay her bills in Birmingham. She worked as a sales clerk at a Parisian department store at the Galleria Mall, but her slim earnings made life difficult. Dabo—who lived in Unit 81 of the Fontainebleau Apartments with a roommate and paid $130 a month in rent—eventually asked his mom to move in with them.

Carol stayed with Dabo. Always inventive, Dabo wedged a broomstick into his closet so his mom would have something to hang her clothes on. Together they shared a queen-sized bed—something they would do for the rest of Dabo's undergraduate career at Alabama. Carol relished this time with her son; he made her feel safe and she didn't have to worry as much about money. Her alarm buzzed at 5:00 a.m. most mornings so she could make the fifty-minute drive to her department store job in Birmingham, but she didn't mind the commute. What mattered was that she was with her son, they both were happy, and they took care of each other—the perfect embodiment of what mothers and sons should do for each other. As for Dabo, seeing his mom work so hard inspired him to drive even harder for a better life, a better future. "It was a little different at first," Dabo said, "but again, you're in the middle of situations in your life, you just make the best of them."

Dabo's friends called her Mama Swinney. Players were known to randomly knock on the door and politely ask if she wouldn't mind doing their laundry, which of course she happily would do. She also sewed when one of Dabo's buddies needed a piece of clothing stitched together and she became famous for her homemade brownies, which never lasted long in Dabo's kitchen.

But the best times were on Sunday nights, when Carol took command of the kitchen. She cooked plateful after plateful of chicken and dumplings, a savory dinner that increased not only Carol's standing among the players but also Dabo's, because his mom always made enough food to fill everyone's stomach and even send them home with leftovers. Then there was a dessert—homemade brownies or peach cobbler—that rivaled anything on the menus of the finest restaurants in the South.

"We all loved Dabo's mom because we got home-cooked meals in college," said Norm Saia, who grew up with Dabo in Pelham and walked onto the team with his buddy. "And Dabo just enjoyed having his mom there. He loved her as much as a son could. He would do anything for her—anything. Some college kids can be a little shy about expressing how much they love their mom or dad. But not Dabo. They had been through so much together. He got his toughness from her. He got his resiliency from her, and he knew it. He was thankful every day that she was his mom, and he wasn't afraid to express that, no matter who was around."

Was it strange for Dabo to share a room and a bed with his mom during college? No, because he learned two fundamental truths at a young age: one, you do anything and everything you can to take care of your family, and two, who really cares what anyone thinks about you and what *you* need to help your family? Everyone has a different normal; Dabo's was just a little *more* different than the typical college student.

DABO IMPRESSED COACHES WITH his work ethic, his effort, and his never-stop, never-quit approach to practice, even when he was trying to block a first-string defensive back who was bigger, stronger and faster than him. Tommy Bowden, the wide receivers coach, was particularly taken with Dabo, his physically underwhelming wide receiver. Years later, Bowden said that there was just something different about Dabo, his confidence and his infectious smile. It seemed to Bowden that nearly every player on the team admired Dabo.

What most of the coaches didn't know was that sometimes after practices, and even games, Dabo would put his leaf blower in the back seat of his car and drive to Birmingham. Once in a well-to-do neighborhood, Dabo parked and knocked on doors, asking strangers if they needed their gutters cleaned— just as he had done in high school. If he was given the green light, Dabo climbed onto the roof with his blower in hand and began clearing out the muck in the gutters. He needed money for rent, books, his credit card debt, tuition, and food. As was the case when he was in high school, many of the people whose gutters he cleaned began expecting him to show up each fall, which he did throughout his time as a student, even when playing football at the University of Alabama.

After the 1989 season—and after Dabo had built a strong rapport with Tommy Bowden—head coach Bill Curry resigned after three seasons, leaving Alabama for Kentucky, which at the time Curry believed was a better job. Curry had compiled a solid record in his three seasons of leading the Crimson Tide (26-10), but he was 0-3 against archrival Auburn and complained of the mistreatment of fans. One year earlier, for example, a disgruntled Tide supporter threw a brick through Curry's office window. Hours before offering his resignation, Curry called a team meeting.

"Men," he said, "I guarantee you will win the national championship. The men in this room are going to do that. I know that, and I'd love to be here for it, but I have become a polarizing factor, and all you're doing is having to defend why this is the guy coaching here, and I don't want you to have to do that. I'm going to extract myself from the situation."

The players were stunned. It was true that Crimson Tide fans had never fully embraced Curry (he had no ties to the legendary Bear Bryant or the school), but the team had gone 10-2 that season and won the SEC. Dabo learned a valuable lesson, one that he would carry with him for years: If you ever coach at a school where your personal connections don't run a mile deep, you must do one thing—one thing that is more important than anything else: Win over the local fan base, especially those boosters with thick wallets and access to the power brokers in the athletic department.

EVERY NEW COACH IN college football wants to bring in his own staff, and Gene Stallings—the man who replaced Curry and who had played for the Bear at Texas A&M and was on Bryant's Alabama coaching staff from 1958 to 1964—was no different. All the assistants under Curry were let go, including wide receiver coach Tommy Bowden, who had been one of Dabo's biggest advocates and one of the few coaches who actually knew his name. The coaching turnover meant that everything Dabo had done up to this point meant nothing. None of the new coaches cared that he had made the team as a walk-on, or survived the hardships of camp, or won over the

heart and mind of Rich Wingo, which was perhaps his greatest accomplishment as an Alabama player. Now he'd have to
prove himself again to a new staff.

During spring practice, the new wide receivers coach, Woody
McCorvey, essentially ignored Swinney, believing he would
never be good enough to play. One of Dabo's first goals that
spring was to simply have McCorvey say his name at least once,
but the coach never did. To illustrate just how much McCorvey
wasn't interested in Dabo, he didn't even play him in the spring
game. Dabo was devastated. If his own position coach wasn't
going to give him a chance, he knew he'd never step onto the
field during an actual game. He briefly considered transferring,
heading to a new school for a fresh start and a fair shot.

But the dream kept stirring in Dabo, the lifelong Bama fan.
The 1990 season started and he kept working, treating every
play on the scout team like it was as important as fourth-
and-one in the closing seconds of a national championship
game. Alabama started the season 0-3, losing to Southern
Miss (27–24), Florida (17–13), and Georgia (17–16). After the
team's fourth loss, a 9–0 defeat to Penn State at Bryant–
Denny Stadium on October 27, Woody McCorvey decided he
needed some fresh blood at wide receiver. The team's top two
wide receivers—Prince Wimbley and Craig Sanderson—had
been injured on consecutive days, and so after the loss to the
Nittany Lions, McCorvey was desperate—so desperate that he
decided to give a walk-on a chance.

Dabo still thought that McCorvey didn't know his name
when, days after the Penn State game, the wide receiver

coach signaled for him during practice to come over for a talk. As Dabo ran at full speed toward McCorvey—it may have been the fastest he'd run since arriving in Tuscaloosa—Dabo thought of all the things he could have done wrong. He wondered if he missed a block, flubbed an assignment, failed to turn in some homework, or maybe he had missed a class. He didn't know, but he definitely expected to be on the business end of an ass chewing in front of the entire team.

Dabo didn't realize it, but McCorvey had been paying close attention to him. McCorvey noticed the effort he gave in practices, his willingness to get plowed over by a bigger, starting player in the hope of making that player better and more prepared for the upcoming opponent. Dabo did the little things—like run from drill to drill, perform pass patterns with precision and enthusiasm even when he knew the ball wouldn't be coming his way. It was clear to McCorvey that Dabo loved football in a way that few players on this team with a 3-4 record did.

McCorvey later said that Dabo always did things "correctly" and was impressed by how he "went about his business." On this day when he summoned Dabo, McCorvey was upset with a few of his top receivers, who had been dropping passes and loafing through practice. McCorvey told Dabo that if he had a good practice, he'd travel with the team to Mississippi State in Starkville, Mississippi, the upcoming Saturday. "Dab, I need somebody who can catch the football," McCorvey said. "If you catch the ball, I'm playing you on Saturday."

Dabo took off running to the locker room, where he put on a white jersey, meaning he was no longer a scout team player.

He sank to his knees and said a quick prayer, thanking God for this chance of a lifetime. Then he lit a blue streak back to the field, running as fast as he could so he could line up with the varsity. Once on the field, he was typical Dabo: He fearlessly blocked bigger players on run plays and ran his pass-play routes with textbook precision. Every cylinder of his internal engine stroked with superb power and control. McCorvey was impressed, but he didn't immediately tell Dabo that he had performed well enough to warrant a spot on the travel squad.

Then the travel roster was posted. Dabo examined it closely and—oh my—there it was: His name and his number. Once every player had a chance to see who was listed on the sheet of paper, Dabo snuck back into the football complex and took it down, wanting to keep it for posterity—and he did. He framed it and it now hangs on a basement wall in his house in Clemson. On the bus ride over to Starkville, no player was happier and more fulfilled than Dabo. He had achieved the re-markable, becoming the blue-moon rare walk-on at Alabama to make the travel team as a sophomore.

The Tide throttled Mississippi State 22–0. Dabo failed to catch a pass, but that didn't dampen his spirits, which for the three hours of the game had soared like a rocket. Two weeks later, against Cincinnati at Legion Field in Birmingham, Dabo caught his first and only pass of the season, a reception that went for 18 yards and a first down.

DABO RARELY RELAXED, TREATING every practice like it was his chance to make a lasting impression on the coaching staff and his teammates. Safety Chris Donnelly, who eventually would live with Dabo and his mom, remembers being in the middle of two-a-days and they were running in tar-bubbling, 110-degree heat. Donnelly looked over at Dabo, who was smiling like he was having the time of his life—a young man who loved the grind almost as much as the games. Flabbergasted, Donnelly said to his buddy, "What world do you live in? Can I live in your world for a little bit?"

Even though Gene Stallings and the Alabama offense rarely threw the ball early in Stallings's tenure, preferring instead to rely on the Tide's vaunted rushing attack and swarming, smothering defense, this conservative style of play perfectly suited Dabo's skill set. He wasn't going to outrun or juke any defensive back in the SEC, but he had a willingness to block that ran as deep as the red clay in central Alabama. It was almost as if physical contact was his drug, according to one teammate, and the only thing that would allow him to get his fix was more, more, and more contact. In college football, blocking always comes down to will as much as skill, and virtually no one on the team displayed more desire to put his body on the line, to hit opposing players, than did Dabo.

After gaining the confidence of his head coach and receivers coach midway through his redshirt sophomore year, Dabo played in four games to finish out the 1990 season. Coach Stallings, learning about Dabo's financial problems and impressed with his overall good-guy demeanor, awarded him a scholarship. Not one player on the roster was surprised when the news spread that Dabo was no longer a walk-on.

The long shot from Pelham, the cherubic-faced player who had been sitting in the stands at Bryant–Denny less than two years later, had made it.

In his junior season, still sharing a room with his mom, who still enjoyed cooking big dinners for his teammates, Dabo played in nine games and caught two passes. He took a camera with him to every game, constantly snapping photos like a tourist on the best vacation of his life, wanting to record every possible moment of his waking dream. His teammates kidded him about the camera, but Dabo didn't care: He wanted as many moments documented as possible so he could one day tell his children he was an Alabama football player. He would use these pictures to explain to them the virtues of hard work and what can happen when you fully apply yourself to the task at hand.

One of Dabo's closest friends on the team was Norm Saia, a defensive lineman from Pelham. As kids, the two were inseparable—just as they were on the Tuscaloosa campus. "We never missed an Alabama game growing up," said Saia, who still lives in Birmingham. "And the thing with Dabo was, he never got down. Even when his home life was a nightmare, he was positive about life. Heck, he even made me do my homework before we could go out and play basketball or throw around the football."

Midway through his college career, Saia was involved in a serious car accident. He broke his pelvis and couldn't walk for months. He moved back to Pelham. One of the few friends to frequently come see him was Swinney, who would drive him around Birmingham to visit old friends and coaches. "Here Dabo was in the middle of his college life, with football a huge priority, and he knew I was going stir-crazy. So he'd come and say, 'Hey, man, let's go for a ride,'" said Saia. "I wouldn't even get out of the car, but just his positive attitude impacted me."

As a senior, Dabo caught four passes for 48 yards. He also excelled on special teams, where his Rudy-like hustle was often hailed by coaches during film review. When Alabama played Miami on January 1, 1993, for the national championship in the Sugar Bowl, Stallings inserted Dabo into the starting lineup as a wide receiver—the first and only start of his college career. This was Stallings's way of rewarding Dabo for his career of hard work and hustle, which Stallings later said had a positive effect on the entire team. The Tide's starting quarterback, Jay Barker, completed only four of thirteen passes for 18 yards in the national title game—none to Dabo—but Alabama defeated the heavily favored Hurricanes 34–13 to capture the school's first national title of the post–Bear Bryant era.

The Tide had capped off the school's eighth perfect season in history. Led by future first-round NFL draft picks Eric Curry (a defensive lineman), John Copeland (a defensive lineman), and Antonio Langham (a cornerback), Alabama's defense intercepted Miami's Heisman-trophy winning quarterback Gino Toretta three times, which led to three Bama touchdowns. At one point, the Tide, boasting the top-ranked defensive in the nation, lined up all eleven defensive players on the line of scrimmage, further confusing Toretta. "That defense was as talented as I've seen," said Toretta. "They got us good that night."

What made the victory even sweeter for Alabama was the amount of trash talking that Miami—winners of four of the previous eight national titles—had done before the game. Days before kickoff, the two teams met at an event in the French Quarter; the Hurricane players used it as a chance to taunt the Crimson Tide players, hurling R-rated verbal spears. "They were right up in our faces, saying us blankety-blanks don't deserve to be on the same field with them," said Alabama running back Derrick Lassic, who would run for a game-high 135 yards. "We just shook our heads. They were out of control."

Perhaps no one enjoyed the victory more than Dabo, surely the longest shot of all the players in either starting lineup. "Dabo was an athletic, possession type of receiver," said Jay Barker, Alabama's starting quarterback from 1992 to 1994, who won more games (thirty-five) than any other quarterback in Crimson Tide history up to that point. "He's been an underdog his entire life. But he worked at it as hard as any-one, both on the field and off the field. He had a coach's mind even back then. He loved talking Xs and Os, even if he wasn't in the game. And in a lot of ways, football was his escape. It got him away from his problems. It took his mind off all the other things that had happened to him. That's one reason why I think he took football so serious and why it mattered so much to him. It just brought him so much joy."

In Dabo's mind, the national championship game was a blurred culmination of everything he had ever wanted. "It was almost like it was in slow motion," he said. "The game was surreal. At that time Alabama folks remember it had been a long time since Alabama had won a national championship. It had been since 1979. It was a big deal. It was the 100th year of Alabama football....I remember there were three or four minutes to go in the game and I came out of the game and I said to myself, 'Well, that's it.' I remember standing on the sideline just literally like a kid soaking it in, like this was the end for me. I mean, unless the Dallas Cowboys were going to call me, I was probably going to be done with football. I said, 'This was going to be my last play.' I had played forever. I had lived my dream. And I just wanted to soak it in. And I really did."

But Dabo wasn't done yet. He noticed that the equipment managers were running the game balls on and off the field. He approached a manager and said, "Hey, I'm a senior. Give me that ball." Once the final whistle blew, he then held on to the ball—high and tight, as if he were running through a tangle of defenders—and sprinted around the field, slapping high fives with players, fans, and whoever else he could touch. "I had that ball locked down," Dabo said. "It was the best ball security you've ever seen."

In one of the local New Orleans papers the next day, there was a picture of Dabo with the ball and star Alabama running back Sherman Williams. Dabo wrote the photographer a letter and asked him to send him a copy, which he did. To this day,

Dabo still has the game ball in his house—one of his most treasured possessions.

After a victory lap around the field, Dabo joined his teammates in the winning locker room. "The joy was unreal, knowing that you got it done," he said. "That's the greatest moment you can experience as a player. Growing up in Alabama, winning the Sugar Bowl is always a dream."

Dabo wandered around the locker room, aglow, feeling more alive than ever. Several teammates remember seeing a half-smile, an almost proud look on his face, as if he was taking one mental snapshot after the another and freezing them in his mind. Years later, on the grainy film of his memory, Dabo would often replay this scene, this moment, remembering in detail what it was like to be a national champion football player.

RARELY ONE TO TAKE a day off from his studies, Dabo was named to the SEC's all-academic team. And yet Dabo believed that he learned as much from football as he did in the classroom. Between the white lines, he figured out who he was, how much he could tolerate, what it meant to be a good man, a good friend, and a good teammate, what the definition of sacrifice was, what the word *work* truly embodied, and the importance of being both persistent and consistent in everything you do—from how you prepare to how you react to winning to how you deal with failure. What he learned on the fields of the SEC and in Tuscaloosa ultimately planted the seeds for all that he would become—as a coach, a man, a husband, and a father.

During his time on campus, Dabo decided to switch majors. For years he had thought he would study to become a pediatrician. He loved the idea of helping children. But then the reality of accomplishing that goal started to sink in: It would require extra years of schooling and a long residency. So he switched his major to commerce and business administration, his goal one day to operate a hospital. Dabo was always good at managing logistics and problem-solving, and this seemed like a job that ideally suited his skill set.

Dabo became the first in his family to graduate. What made graduation day even sweeter was that Ervil was there to watch his youngest boy walk across the stage, dressed in a cap and gown, and receive his diploma. For several years, Dabo kept asking his dad, "Why don't you stop drinking? Why don't you just try? See what happens. Why don't you go to church? Why don't you put all of your problems behind you and start anew?" Dabo was essentially a life coach for his dad, always trying to uplift him, inspire him, and coax him into positive action. Dabo didn't dwell on the past, nor did he forget it. Instead, he focused on the future with Ervil, how enriched his father's life could be if Ervil set himself free from alcohol and lived a sober, honest life—one filled with honor and integrity and love.

Ervil listened to his son, and the two reconciled. For the first time, Dabo truly understood the power of forgiveness. Ervil wasn't perfect—for several years he drank on Tuesdays and Saturdays, and Dabo knew not to call him on those nights when he was acquainting himself with the bottom of the bottle—but he was working on it. Then when Ervil remarried in 1997, he promised his second wife he would quit completely—and he eventually did. He also gave up cigarettes, his other vice.

Ervil started to piece his life back together. With a business partner, he opened a hardware store in Alabaster, Alabama, located not far from Pelham. He and his new wife lived in a trailer behind the store. Still, Dabo's mother, Carol, wanted nothing to do with Ervil—the destruction he had caused in the previous years was just too much to forgive—and Dabo's brother Tracy, who had moved back to Pelham to become a police officer, essentially stayed away from him as well. Dabo's other brother, Tripp, wasn't around, so Dabo was the only one from the family who was there for his dad, encouraging him to choose a different path—a sober path.

After graduating from Alabama, Dabo started working that summer as an intern for a health care company in Birmingham. He wowed his bosses with his knowledge and dedication to the job, and he was offered a full-time position in the fall. As Dabo considered that option, he continued to earn extra money by cleaning gutters in Birmingham. One man whose gutters he worked on, impressed with Dabo's devotion, offered Dabo a job that paid $30,000 a year plus a company car. Dabo said he'd give it some thought.

Late in the summer, though, an offer was made to Dabo that he couldn't refuse. Gene Stallings called and asked Dabo to be a graduate assistant coach. Until that moment, Dabo had never seriously considered coaching as a profession. Yes, he missed football, but he never thought he'd make a career of it. The pay was abysmal for a twenty-something just starting out in the field, and the hours were brutally long. But the more he thought about it, the more Dabo realized he wasn't ready to let go of the game just yet, that its seductive allure still had its grip on him. He also liked the notion of staying in Tuscaloosa and earning his master's degree in business—which Alabama would pay for—while he was a GA doing grunt work for Stallings and other coaches. So Dabo told his old coach that he'd love the chance to be on his staff. The rest of his life would have to wait at least one or two more football seasons.

Kathleen also graduated in the spring of 1993. Aside from a brief breakup, the two had remained boyfriend and girlfriend throughout college, and by that summer, Dabo knew what had to happen. Even though he only earned $498 a month as a graduate assistant on Stallings's staff, Dabo summoned the courage to walk into a jewelry story. "This is the ring I want," Dabo said to a woman behind the counter, pointing to a diamond ring that was priced at $2,800. "Here's what I have," Dabo said. "Here's the check from the university. I will sign it over to you. It's all I got." He then took out his wallet and handed the store clerk the check he'd made as a graduate assistant and also gave her an insurance check for $2,400 to cover the rest of the cost. He didn't know how he'd live the rest of the semester, but he didn't care for two reasons: He was in mad love, and he knew this was the best decision he would ever make.

Now Dabo hatched a plan. On August 19, 1993, he casually asked Kathleen to go out to dinner. Dabo picked her up from her apartment—she was wearing workout clothes—and took her to the Cypress Inn, an iconic local establishment that served Southern family recipes and was nestled along the waterfront of the Black Warrior River on Rice Mine Road East, directly across from the university. As part of his ruse, Dabo told Kathleen throughout dinner that he wanted to earn a bowl bonus in December so he could buy her a ring.

After enjoying their meal together, the two went for a walk to Denny Chimes, the bell tower on the south side of the quad. They strolled hand in hand through the Southern darkness—in love, in no rush—practically disappearing into each other's eyes whenever they glanced at each other. They reached the tower. At 10:00 p.m., bells began to chime, echoing across campus and into the night. Dabo dropped down to one knee and asked Kathleen to marry him. She said yes and they both melted into a puddle of happy tears.

THE NEWLY ENGAGED DABO needed his space. Carol moved out of her son's place and into her own apartment in Tuscaloosa. On her first Valentine's Day alone in the apartment, Carol came home from her job to a red rose, a box of candy, and a card. Inside the card the words read: *Happy Valentine's Day to my #1 V'tine! Thank you for all that you sacrifice to see that I have everything. You are truly a special person to all. I love you, Mom!*

Carol remarried and moved to Birmingham with her new husband, Larry McIntosh, who worked for State Farm. Dabo immersed himself in coaching, working with players who were far more talented than he was. He also observed the coaching staff closely, watching and analyzing all of their behaviors and methods. He compulsively filled up notebook after notebook with ideas, concepts, diagrams, and thoughts on the things Alabama coaches were doing, both good and bad. He kept every notebook.

Dabo and Kathleen married in 1994. Dabo said it felt like he was marrying his sister, given how long the two had known each other and dated. The first few years were difficult financially for Dabo and Kathleen. He was still making less than $500 month as a graduate assistant coach. Kathleen had earned her master's in education and taught school, but they did not live a luxurious life. Their go-to meal was SpaghettiOs. Still, the young couple couldn't have been happier. They had each other, and that was enough, as they were just beginning their married life together.

In February 1996, Dabo's standard two-year apprenticeship as a graduate assistant came to an end. He was now twenty-six years old, a relatively new husband, and a man without a job. He figured he had no chance at landing a full-time position at Alabama, because Stallings rarely hired coaches that young on a full-time basis. But Stallings had been paying close attention to Dabo. There was something about him—to this day, Stallings has trouble describing what this quality was— that was just different. He connected to players in a way that most coaches couldn't, and the players in turn truly listened to Dabo, even though he was a lowly graduate assistant.

Stallings didn't want to lose Dabo, especially to a rival team in the SEC. So the head coach called Dabo into his office and asked him if he'd like to become the wide receivers coach at the University of Alabama. Dabo nearly fell out of his chair. Stallings said he wanted to give young coaches a chance to show what they can do at a school the caliber of Alabama; Dabo happily accepted the job, the $38,000 salary, and the car that went along with it.

For five years, Dabo worked long hours on the Alabama staff. Stallings retired at the end of the '96 season, and Mike DuBose, who had been the Tide's defensive coordinator, replaced him and retained Dabo. The Swinneys started a family—son Will was born on August 19, 1998; son Drew came into the world on January 23, 2000; and son Clay would open his eyes for the first time on July 29, 2003—and the couple couldn't have been happier. For several years, Dabo's home and professional life were as good as he ever could have imagined. But then the whiff of scandal began to envelope the Alabama program—an odor that would grow so strong it would eventually drive Dabo out of coaching.

In January 2001, the *Commercial Appeal* in Memphis published a story that Alabama booster Logan Young paid Lynn Lange, the high school coach of defensive lineman Albert Means, $200,000 to direct Means to Alabama. Lang later testified under oath that he received $150,000 from Young, who eventually was convicted and sentenced to six months in federal prison. The NCAA hammered Alabama: five years' probation, a two-year bowl ban, and lost scholarships. Officials from the

NCAA said in a news conference that they had seriously considered giving Alabama the death penalty, which would have set the football program back for years, if not decades.

Albert Means denied doing anything wrong, and Alabama released him from his scholarship. He finished his career at Memphis. But the Means case, along with Dabo's connection to DuBose, who was embroiled in a scandal with a female secretary (the school paid $350,000 to settle a sexual harassment claim she had filed), left him radioactive. By all accounts, Dabo had not violated any rules or done anything remotely inappropriate, but this was certain: He was guilty by association.

Following the 2002 season, head coach Dennis Franchione told Dabo that his services were no longer needed on the coaching staff. After Franchione bolted for Texas A&M on December 5, 2002—he wanted no part of a program that was hamstrung by the NCAA's punishment—new Tide coach Mike Price called Dabo and asked him if he'd be interested in joining his staff and coaching tight ends. But just before Dabo signed his contract, Price changed his mind, telling Dabo he needed a more experienced coach. He instead hired Sparky Woods, who had coached college football since 1976—when Dabo was seven years old. After a boozy night at a strip club in Pensacola, Florida, Price would never coach a game in Tuscaloosa, but Price's dismissal didn't change the new reality for Dabo:

He was no longer a football coach. His life in the real world—the nine-to-five world, the coat-and-tie world—was about to begin.

CHAPTER 4

DABO IN WILDERNESS

He wasn't worried, not a bit, on that winter day in early 2001 when he packed up his office at the Crimson Tide football facility in Tuscaloosa. As Dabo placed his football life into cardboard boxes—he'd been a player or a coach at Alabama since 1990 and he carefully wrapped and stored each photo and memento from those eleven formative years—he figured head coaches around the country would soon start calling to offer him a job. He even told his wife, "Everybody's gonna want to hire me. I've coached eight years at Alabama. I've won a national championship. I've won an SEC championship. I've recruited all these guys."

Dabo thought Notre Dame might call. The Irish wide receivers coaching position had just opened because Urban Meyer had left to become the head coach at Bowling Green. Dabo's former coach, Gene Stallings, phoned Irish head coach Bob Davie and strongly recommended Dabo, praising his coaching skills, his unique way of connecting with players, and how he took the time away from the field to mold his players into young men of character and substance. Stallings's endorsement couldn't have been more effusive or supportive.

Mal Moore, the Alabama athletic director, also reached out to Davie to vouch for Dabo. As much as anyone, Moore had watched Dabo grow as a coach during his time in Tuscaloosa. He marveled at how easily Dabo established lasting rapport with his players. His wide receivers considered him a big brother they didn't want to let down—and also a mentor they could approach in confidence and confide their worries and fears. There was a bond that existed inside the wide receivers group at Alabama, Moore believed, that was rare and a credit to Dabo.

But Davie was unmoved: He never contacted Dabo or responded to his calls.

Undeterred, Dabo wrote letter after letter to coaches throughout the nation who had openings on their staffs. He received a few polite rejections, but many coaches didn't even bother to respond. He attended the American Football Coaches Association Convention, meeting and greeting and handing out business cards—still no luck, as he was told over and over that he wasn't "the right fit" on different staffs. Dabo even visited the Birmingham Thunderbolts of the short-lived XFL in his quest to find a job in football. But not even the Thunderbolts were interested in Dabo Swinney.

STILL, DABO REMAINED AS hopeful as a sunrise, just as he always did. He planned to take a month or two off, continue to put pen to paper and send out his résumé, and by spring he figured someone would hire him. Of all the problems he had overcome in his life, this seemed a minor obstacle.

Then, as he networked and tried to expand his Rolodex of supporters, he received a call from Rich Wingo, who years earlier had been the Alabama strength coach and had been in charge of the walk-on program under Stallings. Even though Wingo had been hard on Dabo, he deeply admired his former player. Wingo was now the president of AIG Baker Real Estate—a development company in Birmingham—and he hadn't talked to Dabo in about a decade, but he remembered that he was an impressive young man. He recalled that Dabo had a strong religious faith, was family oriented, tough minded, smiled constantly, and acted like he never met a stranger. Wingo figured Dabo would be successful at anything he believed in and put his effort to.

"I really just went to meet him so he wouldn't make me do up-downs or something," Dabo said. "I was scared to death of him. I thought he was in construction. I didn't know anything about shopping centers."

After catching up with his former walk-on player, Wingo cut to the point of the meeting: He offered Dabo a sales job, primarily focused on negotiating leases for retail spaces at shopping centers. Wingo told Dabo that his business was doing well and was growing across the entire country. He emphasized that he wanted Dabo's positive attitude on his sales team.

At first, Dabo wasn't interested in the offer, explaining that he really wanted to get back to coaching and was devoting all of his energy into making that happen. Wingo then told his former player that a coach without a team or a paycheck is, in reality, just a lonely man who is unemployed and not earning a dime. Wingo reminded Dabo of the importance of providing for his wife and his two young children. Wingo then said he could pay Dabo $80,000 a year—more than he had ever made in coaching. After a discussion with Kathleen, Dabo accepted the position.

THERE HE WAS, A boyish-looking thirty-one-year-old walking out the front door of his Tuscaloosa home on a Monday morning in April 2001, decked out in a dress shirt, carrying a briefcase, striding toward his car. He had no clue what he was getting himself into—he had successfully avoided a real-world job for nearly ten years, and he didn't know how to operate a fax machine and wasn't too facile with a copy machine if it required more than a few buttons to be pushed—but Dabo knew one thing: He had to work. Wingo had forcefully reminded him of that. Plus, he figured he'd go stir-crazy if he didn't do something, even if it meant toiling in a job outside of football. He also believed with all his heart that he was going to be the best dadgum shopping center lease agent in America—he was sure of it.

Kathleen stood at the doorway of their house with their two young boys, watching her husband climb into his car for his first day on the job at AIG Baker. She couldn't take her eyes off him as he pulled out of the driveway and disappeared into the distance. A wave of sadness washed over her. She knew that Dabo still wanted to coach, and she felt like his football aspirations had just been shattered. She turned, walked back into the house, and cried.

A few moments later, the phone rang. Kathleen gathered herself and answered. On the other end of the line was the mother of an Alabama player that Dabo had coached. This woman wanted to thank Dabo for all that he had done for her son, transforming him from a wayward kid into a young man of character and class. She hoped to personally tell Dabo how much she admired him, appreciated him, and—yes—loved him. Hearing these touching words, Kathleen broke down again. "He's supposed to be a coach," Kathleen said into the phone. She later commented that seeing Dabo go off to work that first day was like "sending my child off to boarding school."

Alone in his car, Dabo said the same prayer every morning on his way work: He asked his Higher Power to guide him to the person who could give him a coaching job. And if He couldn't do that, Dabo asked God to remove from his heart his desire to coach again.

ON HIS FIRST DAY of work in the business world, Dabo made the fifty-five-mile drive from Tuscaloosa to Birmingham on Interstate 20/59, the same route that two decades earlier his hero, Bear Bryant, had transited during his funeral procession from First United Methodist Church in Tuscaloosa to Birmingham's Elmwood Cemetery. Once Dabo arrived at the

AIG Baker office, briefcase in hand, he was escorted to his desk, which had a phone and computer on it. Dabo took a seat in his chair, put his briefcase down, and for several minutes just stared straight ahead in silence, deep in thought, pondering how his life journey had led him to this time and this place. He wasn't depressed and he wasn't elated—he just needed to pause and reflect before he could begin attacking this latest challenge.

Rich Wingo lumbered over to Dabo's desk and welcomed him to his new career. He handed Dabo two boxes that were filled with papers—one was for a leasing job in Las Vegas and one was for a project in Olathe, Kansas. Wingo told Dabo never to be afraid to ask questions and that he was now the overseer of those two projects. The boss then told his new employee that everyone in the office was there to help him and everyone believed in him. All these years later, Wingo was still Dabo's coach.

Dabo spent his first months learning the ins and outs of the job. He attended shopping center conventions, striking up conversations with anyone who had knowledge of the best ways to lure potential retail clients into the variety of spaces shopping centers and malls offered. He set up business lunches and was always mindful to pen handwritten thank-you notes to anyone who spent time with him. He had business cards printed and handed them out like candy to potential clients. He began to genuinely enjoy his second career. Still, he prayed in his car every morning to return to coaching.

When he wasn't meeting and greeting people in the industry, Dabo studied—and then studied more. The first principle of shopping center leasing is that the most important stores are the big tenants, known as the anchors, such as Walmart, Target, Best Buy, Macy's, or multiplex movie theaters. When cobbling together a list of tenants, these must be the first ones to sign the lease. Then it's the responsibility of the leasing agent to surround the anchors with smaller stores. They could be local or national, but it is generally more difficult to fill these spaces because the risk for the smaller tenant—one who may not have the financial security of a bigger tenant with stores across the country—is far greater. This was Dabo's main charge: convince the smaller tenants to sign leases once the anchor store or stores were secured.

A good leasing agent, Dabo quickly surmised, is like a good recruiter in college football. Having spoken to several successful leasing agents, Dabo learned that he needed to relentlessly pursue potential clients, had to cultivate and nurture relationships, and if he made a promise, he absolutely had to ensure his word was his bond, that his handshake on an agreement was as firm as a signed contract. Within months, he developed a reputation for being a stand-up guy in this subculture of shopping centers. Plus, he prided himself on being overprepared; every time he walked into a meeting, he needed to know more about market research and demographic trends than anyone else in the room.

For every project, he immersed himself in data about traffic counts and income levels of potential customers, trying to learn as much as possible about who would shop at each center. Then he had to figure out what business could flourish with that kind of clientele. He researched possible tenants at different shopping centers, figuring out what was important to them, what they hoped to accomplish, and to what customers they wanted to cater. He then emphasized what he learned about the tenant in his face-to-face meetings with them. "You know you're sitting here with a Super Target and Bed, Bath & Beyond," Dabo would say, "and this is a space that we're going to be able to get you a deal on."

Dabo's first big job was at the shopping center in Las Vegas that Wingo had mentioned on Dabo's first day. He met with several different possible clients, each with different products and customers in mind. He regaled them with a range of deeply researched demographic reports and a variety of relevant historic sales figures with startling ease, all of it tattooed on his near-photographic memory. He articulated his vision for the shopping center, vividly drawing a word picture of architectural and shopper-friendly characteristics. He detailed who would frequent each store and why, and then he'd explain in graphic detail the myriad reasons why the center was destined to flourish. Dabo was, according to a person involved in these meetings, a natural at piecing together deals and succinctly explaining why these were opportunities not to be missed. He eventually filled every space in the Vegas shopping center project.

Dabo always had a way with words, dating back to his time in grade school when he loved to wax on and on about his admiration of all things Crimson Tide. But now as a young adult in the working world, he was really finding his voice. With each professional meeting and each professional interaction he had while at AIG, he became a more seasoned, succinct, lyrical speaker. He learned that the two keys to doing well in all of his business meetings were understanding the needs of the client and then articulating why the client would be making the biggest mistake of his professional life if he *didn't* heed his advice.

Dabo became fond of using folksy, homespun language in his pitches. For instance, he'd tell clients who were contemplating leasing space in one of his shopping centers that anyone can stand on the side of a lake, cast a fishing line into the water, and snag a small fish. This was a simple and safe way of life, using a cane pole, a red-and-white bobber on the line and crickets for bait, to try to catch, say, a sunfish.

But, Dabo would tell customers, if you wanted to land your personal Moby Dick—if you wanted to reel in that great white whale you've been wanting to catch since you were knee high to a grasshopper—then you needed to get into a boat, paddle out to deep waters, and be willing to take a chance on yourself. This was the way to financial glory and this was the path to being successful in life, Dabo would passionately argue, believing that you can always catch that big fish if you're willing to row out where those big fish swim.

It was also the *way* he spoke to potential tenants that made him so successful. Always smiling, always maintaining eye contact, always answering every last question with patience and poise, he put clients at ease with his optimism and energy. Even if a tenant had never met Dabo before, by the end of their first or second meeting—according to several past associates—the tenant was inclined to trust him. They were moved, in effect, to sign a lease with him, even if they had doubts about the opportunity before they sat down with Dabo. This was Dabo's magic.

But not even Rich Wingo believed Dabo would fill out the shopping center in Olathe, Kansas, one of the first projects Wingo assigned his young leasing agent. But in a massive first business success, Dabo did. He sold dreams—and from the very start, he sold them like a man who knew a thing or two about recruiting. Dabo didn't realize it at the time, but he was honing his persuasion skills nearly every time he sat down for a sales pitch—skills that were developing at warp speed.

By his second year of being a shopping center leasing agent—as he traveled the country for meetings with clients, meetings with various city councils to discuss zoning issues, and meetings with property owners to talk about purchasing land—Dabo basically stopped telling people he used to coach football. This was his new life now, and there was no use in looking backward. When he wasn't on the road, he worked from 9:00 a.m. to about 4:30 p.m., five days a week. He relished spending weekends with his wife and their two young boys, being the father he always wanted to be, throwing a football around in their backyard, and just being present in their lives. Plus, he was making more money than he ever thought possible—over $200,000 a year with bonuses.

He and Kathleen started building their 6,400-square-foot dream house on Greystone Drive in Birmingham. Life was settling in for Dabo. At intersections, on vacant lots, and in storefront windows throughout Birmingham emerged signs with white letters on a green background that read CALL DABO SWINNEY. He was making a name for himself, albeit not the way he thought he would when he was on the Crimson Tide coaching staff.

Dabo worked with several former Alabama players who Rich Wingo had known when he was in Tuscaloosa. AIG had a gym and an outdoor basketball court, and it wasn't uncommon for noon pickup basketball games to break out, with many of the former Tide stars charging down the court like they were still in college, including former Bama wide receiver Craig Sanderson, linebacker Jeff Rouzie, and running back Kevin Turner (who was later diagnosed with Amyotrophic Lateral Sclerosis [ALS] and would succumb to the disease, brought on by Chronic Traumatic Encephalopathy [CTE], in 2016).

Dabo became especially close with Turner, who played with him at Alabama and then for eight years in the NFL, where he was known for being one of the best blocking fullbacks in the league. On one business trip, Dabo and Turner hopped in a car together in Birmingham and drove four hours to Anderson, South Carolina, to meet with potential clients. The two had some downtime while in Anderson, so Dabo and Turner headed thirty minutes north to Clemson to check out Death Valley and Memorial Stadium. Dabo hadn't been to Clemson, but he still followed the career of Tigers' head coach Tommy Bowden, who for one season had been his wide receivers coach at Alabama. Dabo enjoyed watching Bowden and Clemson on television on fall Saturdays. And who knew? Maybe Dabo would randomly bump into Bowden on campus and reignite their relationship?

Dabo still wanted to coach; he just didn't tell as many people about that desire as he used to. He missed football so much that it was hard for him just to watch his beloved Crimson Tide on television. During his two-year stint as a leasing agent, he didn't attend a single Alabama game. On game days, with the Tide playing on the living room television, Dabo frequently said to his wife, "I have all this knowledge of football and organization and players and it's being wasted."

During his time at AIG, he was offered a job to be a head coach at a lower-level Football Championship Subdivision school. Dabo called Gene Stallings for advice. Stallings had become a father figure to Dabo, and when Dabo had questions about career decisions, he often turned to his former head coach. "If you take that job, you'll be lost," Stallings told Dabo. "It's going to be tough for you to come back. You need to bide your time and a good job will come around."

Dabo wasn't so sure about that—and neither was Woody McCorvey, who had been Dabo's wide receiver coach for three years at Alabama. Like Stallings, McCorvey loved Dabo like a son, and he genuinely worried that Dabo's days on the sideline could be over. The problem for Dabo, as McCorvey saw it, was that he simply didn't have many personal relationships and connections with coaches currently in the profession.

Dabo had spent his entire career at Alabama, and his only two head coaching mentors—his coaching rabbis—were Stallings and Bill Curry. McCorvey made calls on Dabo's behalf and told any coach who would listen that Dabo would be an asset to their staff, but McCorvey too often got the sense from other coaches that Dabo was somehow involved in the problems that had caused Alabama to nearly get the death penalty from the NCAA. He was, in other words, damaged goods.

But Dabo still prayed for God to put someone in the path of his life that could help him return to football. On that business trip to Anderson, South Carolina, with Kevin Turner, the pair drove to the east side of Memorial Stadium and walked inside. Dabo was in awe, euphoric at being back at a college football stadium once again. He took a picture of Howard's Rock, which he'd only seen on television, and then gazed slowly, left and right, reveling at the sight of the lush, pristine green field. The shopping center leasing agent felt like he was at a very special place. Overcome with joy, he did what he normally did when emotion filled his heart: He called his wife.

"You're never going to believe where I am!" Dabo said excitedly over the phone to Kathleen. "Kevin and I just drove over to Death Valley! To Clemson! It's so cool!"

Dabo's final project as a leasing agent was in 2003 at a shopping center in a Birmingham suburb. He had $100 million worth of leases to get signed. He convinced clients from businesses as varied as Panera Bread, Sumo Japanese Steakhouse, and Zoës Kitchen—to name a few—that this shopping center would unlock untold profits for them and that it was time for them to jump into the waters where the big fish swim. They all agreed.

Dabo's two-year foray into the world of business was vital to his growth as a person and—yes—as a coach. It gave him insight into the culture of business and the characteristics that make business leaders successful. He saw how a large company was structured, how the day-to-day operation flowed, how to win over skeptical clients, how big decisions by the CEO were made, and how a good CEO earned the respect and admiration of his employees.

His two years at AIG also made Dabo realize that he didn't need football as much as he thought he did. He now knew that he could provide a nice life for his family even if he never coached another day in his life. He understood that if he were to go back to coaching, he'd be subject to being fired— he'd already experienced that—and now he had something to cushion that potential setback, which provided a great sense of relief. Given that he had flourished in business, the pressure to succeed in football—if he returned—wouldn't be as great, because now he had a plan B, a fallback.

YEARS EARLIER, IN 1998, when Dabo was the wide receivers coach at Alabama, he heard that his old coach Tommy Bowden was going to be back in Alabama and speaking at First Baptist Church in Tuscaloosa. Bowden was in his final year of coaching at Tulane, and Dabo wanted to reconnect with him. So, on a Sunday morning, Dabo and Kathleen sat side by side in a church pew to hear Bowden talk from the pulpit. After the service, a crowd enveloped Bowden. Dabo waited for the mass to thin before he approached Bowden. After making small talk, Dabo told Bowden about his life and his desire to climb the coaching ladder. The conversation lasted only a few minutes. The two men then parted ways. Bowden returned to Tulane, and the next day Dabo was back at the Alabama football facility.

Fast-forward five years. On a Friday in January 2003, a secretary at AIG buzzed Dabo's intercom and said that Mr. Tommy Bowden was on the line. Bowden had recently completed his fourth season at Clemson—the Tigers finished 7-6 and lost to Texas Tech 55–15 in the Tangerine Bowl. Now Bowden recalled that long-past conversation he had had with Dabo at the First Baptist Church in Tuscaloosa. He was impressed then with Dabo and remained so five years later.

Once the two were connected, hellos were quickly exchanged and then Bowden got to the point: He said that his wide receivers coach had decided to leave Clemson for another job and he wanted to know if Dabo might be interested in interviewing for it. "*Why me?*" Dabo asked. Bowden told his former player that he thought he could really help his team in recruiting.

Bowden told Dabo he should come to Clemson and at least meet with him and his staff. Dabo agreed. Before he arrived, Bowden called Wingo. They had coached together at Alabama and had remained friends. "How much is Dabo making?" Bowden asked.

"Forget it," Wingo said, laughing. "I'm not telling you a thing." Wingo vigorously endorsed Dabo for the job.

Dabo checked in with his wife. "What do you think about moving?" he asked.

The Swinneys were about a month away from moving into their new house. Naturally, Kathleen thought her husband was referring to their new place on Greystone Drive, so she said she was excited.

"No," Dabo said. "What do you think about moving to Clemson?"

Dabo flew into Clemson for his interview. One of the first signs he saw after he landed in Greenville, South Carolina, was Pelham Road. Dabo—who grew up in Pelham, Alabama—had always been a believer that his Higher Power threw little hints at him that helped make big decisions in his life, and he took this as a literal sign that Clemson was the place he needed to be.

Once in the Tiger football facility, Dabo talked with assistants, chatted with Bowden, and tried to figure out if this was the right move for him. He had to consider his family. At AIG, he had a stable, good-paying job and was able to spend quality time with his wife and kids. At Clemson, he would be walking into an environment where the head coach's job status was tenuous—the fan base was furious with Bowden for that blowout loss in the Tangerine Bowl to the Red Raiders and their quarterback Kliff Kingsbury—and Bowden could be fired at any time, which in turn meant that the assistants could be fired at any time. Dabo had been through that difficult experience before, and he didn't want to be constantly uprooting his family. For Dabo, this was far from a no-brainer.

And yet the opportunity was precisely what Dabo had prayed for every morning on his drive to work, a chance to return to the profession he loved. Of course there was risk, but the reward could be exquisite—he could be truly happy again in his professional life. It wasn't that he didn't enjoy working as a shopping center leasing agent—he did—but it didn't come close to sating his professional hunger and fulfilling his life's ambition the way coaching did, the way practices did, the players did, the recruiting did, the game days did.

Being back in a building that housed offices occupied by college football coaches felt right to Dabo. He believed that he fit in well with the assistants and support staff he had just met for the first time, but then again, this was an art that Dabo had spent the last two years mastering, connecting with people he had only known for minutes in a deep and meaningful way. After giving it more and more thought, Dabo came to believe that Tommy Bowden was the man he had been praying for. Bowden never even asked Dabo why he had been out of the game for two years.

Dabo wasn't the only candidate being interviewed for the job. Bowden also was interested in T.J. Weist, who had played wide receiver for Bowden when he was at Alabama and was currently the offensive coordinator at Western Kentucky. Weist had more experience than Dabo and, based on his résumé, appeared more football ready. But Dabo had done something remarkable during his quick visit to Clemson: He had won over the Tiger staff. When Bowden polled his coaches about who they thought he should hire, Dabo won in a landslide, with the main reason being that he brimmed with personality and had connected with each and every one of the staff. A few remarked that Dabo was easy to converse with and that he seemed genuinely interested in their lives. Among the staffers, it was quickly taken as an article of faith that Dabo would be pure gold on the recruiting trail.

Days later, Dabo stood in the driveway of his new Birmingham mansion with his homebuilder when his cell phone rang. On the other end of the line was Bowden, the son of Florida State coach Bobby Bowden, who would compile more wins (377) than any coach other than Penn State's Joe Paterno. The elder Bowden possessed many of the same characteristics of a young Swinney—they both were folksy storytellers who loved to talk about any subject at any time of the day. Even though Tommy was more reserved and plainspoken than his famous father, he sure could see a little bit of his dad in Dabo.

Once he got Dabo on the phone, Tommy Bowden offered him the job. Dabo said yes. Bowden later revealed that he likely never would have hired Dabo if he hadn't taken the time to hear him speak at First Baptist Church in Tuscaloosa.

AS DABO AND FAMILY packed up their belongings and their life in Alabama to move to Clemson, Dabo made sure to bring along the architectural blueprints of the dream house he was just finishing building in Birmingham. He planned to construct an identical mansion in his new home in Clemson. Know this about Dabo: When he loves something—when he *truly* loves something—he will not let go of it.

On March 17, 2003, Bowden announced Dabo's hiring in an eight-paragraph press release that mostly detailed Dabo's background, without mentioning that he had been leasing real estate for the previous two years. "[Dabo's] resume as a recruiter is most impressive," Bowden said. "He signed 30 players in his career at Alabama."

At Clemson, Bowden received several emails from coaching friends telling him that he was flat out nuts for hiring a guy who had been out of football for two years. But Bowden was adamant that Dabo would quickly assert himself as not just one of the best recruiters on his staff, but also as one of the top in the nation. The way Bowden viewed it, Dabo's previous two years in real estate had honed—not hindered—his ability to sway young high school kids.

Dabo's experiences as a shopping center leasing agent would always stay with him. Today the sign CALL DABO SWINNEY hangs in his garage, not far from a box of business plans and property files. The keepsakes from his past are a constant reminder of a valuable life lesson that Dabo is quick to share with nearly anyone:

Never give up.

CHAPTER 5

DABO COMES BACK TO CAROLINA

On an otherwise ordinary workday in March 2003, Bill D'Andrea, a senior associate athletic director at Clemson, took a phone call that would change the course of Clemson Tiger football history. If there was a genesis moment in the birth of a twenty-first-century football dynasty—a program that in just over a decade would rival Alabama for supremacy of the sport—this was it.

On the other end of the line was Danny Pearman, who had played tight end at Clemson from 1985 to 1987. D'Andrea had been an assistant coach for the Tigers during Pearman's playing days, and the two had remained friends. On this day, Pearman, now an offensive tackles coach at Virginia Tech, wanted to tell his old coach about a young man named Dabo Swinney who was living in Alabama.

Pearman knew Dabo well. The two had spent seven years together in Tuscaloosa when Dabo was both a player and a coach. Pearman—who had been an assistant coach at Alabama from 1991 to 1997—gushed over the phone to D'Andrea about Dabo, going on and on about how different Dabo was, how he was able to forge deep, meaningful relationships with his players, and how his receivers played their hearts out for him. Pearman told D'Andrea that Dabo had been out of football for about two years, and now he was interviewing for the wide receivers coaching job at Clemson. This was the first time that D'Andrea had ever heard of this thirty-three-year-old former coach at Alabama, and he listened intently as Pearman rhapsodized about Dabo, about his tough background, his agile mind, and his aw-shucks demeanor. Pearman swore to D'Andrea that Dabo would be a perfect fit at Clemson. Without ever saying a word to him, Dabo now had an advocate in D'Andrea, which in a few years would factor in a decision that would radically alter Clemson's football fortunes.

IN THE SPRING OF 2003, ever since his telephone conversation with Danny Pearman, Bill D'Andrea grew intrigued with Dabo. He wanted to see for himself just what kind of coach he was and how he interacted with the staff and his players. So not long after Dabo was hired, D'Andrea asked Terry Don Phillips, Clemson's first-year athletic director, to come with him to watch spring practice. There, on the sideline, D'Andrea often leaned in close to his boss and advised, "Make sure you look over there and watch the receivers and watch Dabo."

The two power brokers at Clemson would then lock eyes on Dabo. He challenged players. He got into their faces and yelled instructions. No detail was too extraneous or too small. He explained and explained again the right way to do everything. But rather than merely telling players what to do, he *showed* them how to run various routes and perform certain drills. Talking, yelling was secondary to demonstrating, teaching, and displaying what he wanted by running the routes and doing the drills himself and then having the players mimic what he had just shown them. All football players—in college and the NFL— more than anything want to get better. After a few practices, improvements by wide receivers on the roster were clearly evident.

Once practice ended, Dabo would often put his arm around his players and tell them how much he cared for them. Phillips and D'Andrea kept their eyes on Dabo. They didn't expressly say it, but Dabo embodied the philosophy of Bear Bryant, who believed in "coaching them hard and hugging them harder." The influence of the Bear, who Dabo had worshipped as a kid and never missed watching his Sunday afternoon television show, was unmistakable.

Dabo had a difficult task from day one. He was replacing Rick Stockstill, an assistant coach for over a decade and a legend at Clemson. Stockstill was known as an elite recruiter— especially in Florida—and a superb developer of talent. The only reason he left the staff was to take a promotion as the offensive coordinator at East Carolina.

In recent years, the Tigers had put plenty of players in the NFL—in 1999, Clemson had six players drafted and in 2001 wide receiver Rod Gardner was picked No. 15 overall by Washington—but the team hadn't finished higher than ninth in the final AP Poll since 1988. Clemson also hadn't won an ACC title since 1991, when head coach Ken Hatfield led the Tigers to a 9-2-1 record. Despite boasting rosters that featured NFL talent season after season, the program had underachieved for years. It was part of Dabo's duty to make sure this trend changed.

Before Dabo's first practice, the players were skeptical of him. They knew that he had hawked real estate the last few years, and many thought there wasn't much of anything this guy could teach them. Dabo was well aware that the first thing he needed to do was prove to the players he was competent and more than ready to do the job. If he didn't earn their respect, he knew he wouldn't last long at Clemson. Some of the wide receivers believed Dabo would be "road kill," as one player put it, as soon as they got out onto the field.

Once Dabo stepped onto the field, the magic began quickly: He helped ordinary players improve, whether it was in doing a little thing like perfecting a blocking drill or a big thing like improving catch radius. Only a few practices into the second act of Dabo's coaching career, his players started to gravitate toward the man, carefully listening to his advice, taking to his coaching. After a few weeks, players could be seen hanging out in his office, talking not only about football, but also about life, girlfriends, or whatever was on their minds.

Phillips and D'Andrea—athletic director and associate athletic director—watched it all.

And it was extraordinary.

FOR DABO, THERE WAS a downside to coaching and it was at times devastating: He had far less time to spend with his family. Back when he was at AIG in Alabama and carrying a briefcase filled with business plans to work each morning, Dabo had most of his nights and weekends free. He could spend hours with Kathleen and the boys. But now that he was back in the grind of coaching, his time was no longer his own—his time now belonged to Clemson first and his family second.

Dabo tried to be as engaged as possible with his three sons. His two older boys sometimes attended practices, watching their dad from the sidelines, filled with pride that their father was a college football coach. Kathleen was something of a maternal figure to the wide receivers who were under Dabo's wing, bringing them home-cooked sweets and asking them about their families. She didn't know it, but she was now in training for a larger role at Clemson almost as much as her husband was.

Because of the long hours at the office, the practices, the competitive football season, and the extended recruiting trips, Dabo started to miss events and games in which his older boys, now in grade school, were participants. Dabo wanted his kids to have as much of a normal life as possible, given how traumatic and transient his own late childhood had been. But now that he couldn't be the dad he aspired to be, he nearly walked away from coaching.

The low point came when Dabo was in Florida trying to convince a high school player to come to Clemson. He called Kathleen that evening to get an update on how the day had gone for the kids. She told him that Will had hit a homerun in his baseball game and was very proud of himself; Drew played with friends and didn't want their fun to stop; and baby Clay, well, he was currently pitching a fit and crying. It was a typical family day in the Swinney household—the kind of day that was a thing of beauty to Dabo.

The fact that Dabo the dad was missing these kinds of family activities broke his heart. He had been away from his wife and three boys for about a month—either in his office, his head buried in paperwork late into the night, or out on the recruiting trail—and now Dabo lost it. The last thing he wanted was to be an absent father. He told his wife, "Kath, I can't do this anymore."

As soon as Dabo returned home, he gathered his boys on his bed. He lovingly looked at them and the words then flowed—words from a man who didn't want to repeat the sins of his own father. "Listen," Dabo said, "I just want y'all to know, y'all are the most important thing in the world to me. I love y'all, and your dad can do a lot of things. And I'm going to get out of coaching and I'm going to get a job where I can coach your teams and be home on the weekends."

The boys looked at their father, confused and concerned. One of his sons said, "But, Daddy, if you're not a coach, we won't get to know the players and we don't get to ride the bus."

Another son said, "Dad, we love you being a coach. And Mom videos anyway." It was true: Kathleen shot videos of his children's events that Dabo missed. Then, often with his kids by his side on the couch, Dabo would watch his sons' sporting events or activities that he hadn't seen in real time. It was fun for the boys to relive the action again, often offering their own commentary and analysis to their dad. More than anything, though, the father-sons talk showed the boys how much he had missed them and how deeply he cared for them.

This on-the-bed conversation with his boys was a life-changing moment for Dabo. He had been fully prepared to quit coaching, but now he realized that he could be a great coach and a great dad. He started to think of all the things he *could* do with his kids because he was coach, rather than focusing on the things he *couldn't* do with them because of his job. He started bringing them around the office more for dinner, to practice more, on Friday nights to the Hilton Garden Inn in Anderson, South Carolina, the team hotel where the team stayed before home games. And he always made time to watch the videos that Kathleen had taken. In this moment on the bed, he finally realized that he needed to cherish and embrace and appreciate what he had—not focus on what he was missing.

This was one reason why the Clemson football offices, in a few years, would become a playground for kids.

ON NOVEMBER 1, 2003, Clemson traveled to Winston-Salem, North Carolina, to play Wake Forest. At the time, Clemson was 5-3 while the Demon Deacons were 4-4. The Tigers were heavily favored, and no one knew better than Bowden that the quickest way to get fired as Clemson's head coach was to lose to Wake Forest. That's exactly what happened in the final season of earlier Tiger coaches such as Ken Hatfield, Tommy West, and Red Parker. The Demon Deacons were the one team on the Clemson schedule that the Tiger fans demanded be demolished each and every season. If Clemson fell short in this game on this autumn afternoon in 2003, the coaches knew Bowden could be forced to walk to the gallows and be fired, which in turn could likely mean all the assistants would lose their jobs. That cold realization had a startling impact on Dabo, who was only coaching in the ninth game of his first year on the Tiger staff.

Within minutes of the ball flying through the air to open the game at just past 3:30 p.m. EST, the outcome seemed preordained. Nothing worked on offense, defense, or special teams for the Tigers. By the end of the third quarter, it was a full-on bloodbath, with Wake Forest leading 45–0. The Demon Deacons ended up obliterating Clemson 45–17, one of the most embarrassing defeats in the school's history.

Dabo didn't ride on a team bus back to Clemson. Instead, wanting to spend time with his family who had come to the game by car, Dabo drove home with Kathleen and their three boys. For four hours, steering the car through the Southern darkness, Dabo didn't have much to say—a rarity for him. He quietly reflected on the state of his life. Just months earlier, he had left a stable and stout salary in Alabama. He had left behind family and friends. He had left a beautiful house. Yes, he had prayed and prayed for this chance to coach again, but what if the decision he recently made was in fact the wrong one? He feared that the entire Clemson coaching staff was on the verge of being let go. Then what would he do? Go home to Alabama and ask Rich Wingo for his job back? Try to find another gig in coaching and move his family for the second time in less than a year? As the miles clicked off the odometer, these questions haunted Dabo like ghosts in the night.

Dabo and Kathleen's new house at 104 Sycamore, the one that was a replica of what they had built in Birmingham and was only five minutes from campus, was about to be finished. A few days after losing to Wake Forest, the homebuilder asked Dabo, "I don't really know how to put this. But if things don't go well, I've got a lot of people that want to buy this house."

"I don't know if we're getting fired," Dabo said. "But I know I'm moving into this house...for a couple of months anyway."

Dabo's fear of being fired was allayed the following Saturday against Florida State. Clemson athletic director Terry Don Phillips had essentially decided that, if the Tigers lost to the third-ranked Seminoles at home, he would fire head coach Tommy Bowden. But Phillips never had to wield the ax and have that difficult conversation with Bowden. Playing its best game of the season in the Bowden Bowl, Clemson beat Florida State 26–10. Tommy Bowden—and Dabo—were safe.

For now.

ON MOTHER'S DAY THE following year, 2004, Dabo called his stepmother and told her the news: He was moving her and Big Erv—whom Dabo had long ago reconciled with—out of the trailer they had lived in for seventeen years and into the

6,400-square-foot house he had built in Birmingham. Telling his dad that he was now providing for him was one of the happiest moments of Dabo's life.

And, continuing to promote a theme now many years in the making, Dabo urged Erv to forsake both the bottle and the smokes. Three years later, Big Erv finally honored his son's wishes and his promise to his second wife, Phyllis: He quit smoking and drinking.

Dabo was oh-so proud. The skills that had made him such a talented recruiter—his charm, his relentlessness, his optimism for the future—had finally taken hold and guided Ervil to the light that Dabo wanted him to see. It wasn't always easy for Erv, but like his son, once he committed to something, he was going to fight like heck to honor what he had promised. And so Big Erv did, never again picking up a drink or taking a drag for the rest of his life. This was the most important sales job of Dabo's life.

RECRUITING WAS DABO'S SIGNATURE skill. He was a good coach—everyone on the Alabama and Clemson staff attested to that—but he was an elite recruiter. And it was his pursuit of one player that would ultimately change the path of Dabo's career and the future of Clemson football.

Dabo met running back C.J. Spiller in 2005. Dabo had traveled to Union County High School in Lake Butler, Florida, to speak with Kevin Alexander, a linebacker who had scholarship offers from Auburn, Tennessee, Maryland, and Louisville. But as Dabo watched tape of Alexander, he became more focused on his teammate C.J. Spiller. Dabo viewed hours of film featuring the talented tailback. His play mesmerized and seduced him. Spiller possessed all the ingredients: agility, cutting ability, boundless raw power, and breakaway sprinter speed. He was the kind of player Clemson had never had in the Bowden era, a player whose singular talent could change the fortunes of the Clemson program.

But Dabo—now also the team's recruiting coordinator—didn't have an appointment to meet with Spiller, then a junior at Union County High. With nothing to lose, Dabo asked a staff member at Union County if he could talk with Spiller, who at the time was in class. The staff member entered Spiller's classroom and said, "The coach from Clemson wants to see you and talk to you." Within minutes, Spiller and Dabo were chatting in the field house.

Dabo asked Spiller if he'd come to Clemson for a recruiting visit. Spiller—impressed by this smiling, brazen, confident young coach—said yes. To make sure that Spiller wouldn't back out, Dabo grabbed his wallet and plucked out a business card. On the back he wrote a short, to-the-point contract. It read: *I, C.J. Spiller, agree to visit CU on the 13th of January.* Dabo told Spiller, *I want to make sure you're going to follow through.* Spiller signed the card contract.

Virtually every school in America wanted Spiller, who most recruiting services ranked as the top overall prospect in perennially talent-rich Florida. In his senior season, he rushed for 1,840 yards and thirty touchdowns. Urban Meyer at Florida went after him hard, telling Spiller that he could be the first great back of his coaching regime in Gainesville. Florida State coach Bobby Bowden, the father of Tommy, tried to lure him to Tallahassee, describing to Spiller how he could help the Seminoles win ACC titles—Florida State was the reigning conference champ—and national titles.

Spiller honored his "contract" with Dabo and traveled to Clemson for a recruiting visit. Dabo proceeded to cast a spell over the running back, telling him how special Clemson was, how the program was growing, how he would be a building block and be a part of something special. Spiller toured the campus, spent time with other running backs on the team, and was taken with the beauty of Death Valley. The day before Spiller returned to Florida, he found Dabo and told him, "I'm about 99 percent sure I'm coming to Clemson."

About a month before National Signing Day, Dabo and Tommy Bowden visited Spiller in his Florida home. Dabo again turned on the charm, assuring Spiller's mom—who didn't visit Clemson with her son, the only school he was considering that she hadn't personally seen—that he would always be there to take care of her son, as would his wife, Kathleen. Clemson was family, Dabo said, and there basically wasn't anything he wouldn't do for a member of his family.

The days passed and still Spiller hadn't formally committed. Dabo kept pressing him, and Spiller made it sound like he was coming to Clemson, but he also wasn't quite ready to make an announcement. Then, in late January, Tommy Bowden called Spiller and told him he was about to step on a plane and fly to Mississippi to see three-star running back

Terry Grant, who Bowden made clear was close to committing to Clemson. "Listen," Bowden said, "are you coming to Clemson?"

"Coach," Spiller replied, "do not get on that plane. I'm coming to Clemson."

"Okay," Bowden said. And just like that, Dabo and Bowden had secured the most important Clemson recruit in at least two decades. (Grant ended up signing with Alabama and played running back for the Tide from 2006 to 2009.) Why was the signing of Spiller so significant? Because it opened the floodgates, showing elite prospects that Clemson was a viable option, a school that would soon compete with the likes of Florida, Florida State, and Alabama for national championships. Spiller's signing helped Dabo sell the Clemson vision to quarterback Tajh Boyd in 2009. It played a role in signing wide receiver Sammy Watkins in 2011. And it conveyed the message to elite high school players from California to Connecticut that Clemson was once again on its way to becoming a serious player in college football.

CLEMSON'S 2006 SEASON ENDED with four defeats in their final five games. The losing was especially difficult for Spiller, then a freshman. He could have gone to practically any school in the country, and now here he was on a team that figured out a new way to lose each week. He was so upset that he weighed transferring to Florida. The Gators had just won a national championship, and Urban Meyer had spent hours recruiting Spiller while he was in high school. During a break from school during his freshman year, Spiller traveled to Gainesville and walked around the Florida campus. He spoke at length with quarterback Tim Tebow. Spiller made a silent vow that he would leave Clemson and become a Gator.

He returned to Clemson and started packing. Yet Dabo didn't give up on his player—Dabo never gives up on anything. He sweet-talked Spiller into going for a ride in his car, which meant Dabo had a captive audience of one. That was when he was at his best.

Dabo talked to Spiller about things not always going the way you want in life, and the frustrations this could cause. He said that he had learned long ago never to make critical, life-altering decisions when his judgment was clouded by frustration. "You just bloom where you're planted," Dabo said. "Why go in somebody else's backyard when you can have your own backyard?"

Dabo spoke in vivid metaphors and parables—a gift of his—and the words resonated with Spiller. The running back with one foot out the door suddenly had a change of heart. He was going to bloom where he was currently planted. He was going to stay at Clemson and he was going to do everything in his power to become the best player he could be while trying to be a role model for others.

Dabo had become a big brother to Spiller, and he meant it when he told players like Spiller that they were part of his family. Dabo reinforced that mantra during spring break of Spiller's freshman year. Driving the family minivan, Dabo took his wife and kids to Florida. They made a pit stop at

Spiller's house, where they spent quality time with C.J. and his family. At one point, Spiller held baby Clay Swinney in his arms and fed him a bottle of warmed milk. That seemingly inconsequential act reinforced Spiller's judgment of Dabo: He was a man of his word. His recruits, his players—they *were* his family.

This theme—*family, family, family*—would soon become the cornerstone of all that would be built at Dabo's Clemson. Spiller would go on to become an All-American and the ninth overall pick in the 2010 NFL draft.

THE NEWS TRAVELED ACROSS the college football landscape, as if pushed by a powerful wind. As Dabo landed elite recruit after elite recruit, his reputation grew at warp speed. In 2006, Rivals.com named Dabo the nation's fifth best recruiter among all assistant coaches. "Ever since I knew Dabo at Alabama, he always had a way of convincing you to see things his way," said Jay Barker, who played quarterback at Alabama and was on the Tide team with Dabo for two seasons. "Even if it was just where we were going to go for dinner, it always seemed like we were doing what Dabo wanted to do. He wasn't pushy about it or insistent. It was just that before you knew it, you were seeing things his way and agreeing with him. He has a natural gift for connecting with people—even people he doesn't know—and then getting people to view things the way he views them. It's really something."

Dabo didn't necessarily want to leave Clemson—his life was good in the sleepy little town of 16,000, and his family enjoyed the slower pace of life—but he also wanted to keep marching up the coaching food chain. In December 2006, as Clemson was preparing to play Kentucky in the Music City Bowl, Rich Rodriguez was nearing a deal to become the head coach at Alabama. Rodriguez, who at the time was the head coach at West Virginia, was finalizing his contract to replace Mike Shula in Tuscaloosa and he wanted Dabo to join his staff.

"Every single coach in the country, especially those of us in the South, knew that Dabo was a special, special recruiter," said Rodriguez. "He consistently got guys that you never thought in a million years would go to Clemson. What can you say? He has a gift." Dabo was ready to accept the offer from Rodriguez and return to Tuscaloosa, but at the last minute Rodriguez opted to turn down Alabama and stay in Morgantown. "I'm the guy who said 'no' to Alabama before they hired Nick Saban," said Rodriguez years later, laughing. "How stupid am I? But I guess you could say I played some sort of role in Nick ending up in Tuscaloosa and going on to win a national championship basically every other year he was there."

As Crimson athletic director Mal Moore continued to search for a new coach after Rodriquez spurned him, another school in Alabama expressed interest in Dabo. The head coaching position at the University of Alabama–Birmingham (UAB) had opened up after Watson Brown resigned, and Dabo was a finalist for the job—a position he desperately wanted. He prepared for his interview like he was cramming for a final exam.

He had a detailed, step-by-step plan for building UAB into a power, and he documented his vision on reams of paper, which he organized into a binder. He developed slogans such as "Blazer Nation!" and genuinely believed that he was the ideal candidate for the job. But then he received a phone call from the school's interim athletic director Richard Margison, who told Dabo that he was canceling the interview because the school had decided to hire Neil Callaway, an assistant at Georgia. Dabo was crushed. Margison said he chose Callaway because "he knows how to win"—an underhanded jab at Dabo's lack of experience.

Days later, on January 3, 2007, Nick Saban was hired at Alabama. Saban didn't personally know Dabo, but he was well aware of his recruiting prowess. Saban often says that it's the horses—not the jockeys—that are the keys to success in college football, which means that players are far more important than coaches. And to get the best players, Saban knew he needed the best recruiters. Shortly after he took the job in Tuscaloosa, he offered Dabo the wide receivers coaching position as well as the title of passing game coordinator if he would return to his alma mater and join Saban's staff. He also offered him a substantial pay raise: $230,000 a year that could reach $300,000 if certain incentives were met. Dabo's salary at Clemson was $135,000.

Dabo was torn. His coaching idol, Bear Bryant, famously said in 1958 that he left Texas A&M to coach at Alabama— where Bryant had played—because "Mamma called. And when mamma calls, you just have to come runnin'." Now mama was calling Dabo, and the lure of Tuscaloosa was strong. It was where he spent the happiest years of his life, where he had matured into a man, where he asked his wife to marry him, where he had started his family, and where his coaching career had taken root.

But Dabo didn't have a personal connection to Saban—the two had never met before Saban was hired at Alabama—and Dabo had already secured the commitments of six players at Clemson that he had personally recruited. He didn't want to abandon those players—walking out on the family was a cardinal sin for Dabo—so he eventually told Bowden that he would remain at Clemson if the school would extend his contract. Bowden was elated. He not only added a few years to Dabo's contract but he also convinced the athletic director to give Dabo a pay raise. What was more, Bowden elevated Dabo to the position of associate head coach, a title that Bowden made up. He had already awarded Brad Scott the title of assistant head coach, so he couldn't give Dabo that. "I had associate head coach [available]," Bowden said. "Don't ask me what that is." Regardless, it was enough to keep Dabo in Clemson and for him to say no to Nick Saban, an answer few coaches or prospects have ever uttered to the man.

ALABAMA AND CLEMSON FACED each other at the start of the 2008 season in the inaugural Chick-fil-A Kickoff Game, a neutral site matchup held in Atlanta at the Georgia Dome; it was a marquee game that was intended to goose TV ratings for college football's opening weekend. Clemson, ranked ninth in the country, was loaded with talent. That summer, college football writers across the country penned story after story about how the Tigers were poised to win their first ACC title in seventeen years. Clemson boasted arguably the best running back tandem in the nation in C.J. Spiller and James Davis. They had elite wide receivers in Jacoby Ford and Aaron Kelly. And they returned a solid quarterback in Cullen Harper. The Crimson Tide, ranked No. 24, was in year two of the Saban era and was still packing its roster with up-and-coming players like freshman running back Mark Ingram Jr. and freshman wide receiver Julio Jones.

The game wasn't close: Alabama thrashed the Tigers 34–10, a butt-whipping that announced Saban meant business at Alabama a year after the Tide had finished 7-6. Worse for Clemson, Bowden became a national punch line. Even though he had C.J. Spiller and James Davis on the roster, he had promised the first carry of the season to true freshman tailback Jamie Harper, a pledge that Bowden had made to convince him to come to Clemson. South Carolina coach Steve Spurrier publicly mocked Bowden's recruiting promise, and it turned into a disaster for Clemson: On the Tigers' second play from scrimmage, Jamie Harper was handed the ball and promptly fumbled. Alabama recovered and turned the fumble into a field goal and an early lead. It was a gut-punching harbinger for the Tigers.

And what about that vaunted Clemson rushing attack? The Crimson Tide outrushed the Tigers 239 to...0. "We got whipped about every way you can get whipped," Tommy

Bowden said after the game. "Obviously, we're not the ninth best team in the country." Cullen Harper, Clemson's quarterback, later said that the shellacking at the hands of Saban and Alabama had shaken the team to its core and "really hurt our confidence."

Kathleen Swinney walked out of the Georgia Dome with Linda Bowden, Tommy's wife. There was a sadness in Linda's eyes. This game confirmed that the sun was just starting to rise on the Saban dynasty at Alabama. His roster was flush with young talent, and Saban—heralded for having signed the nation's top recruiting class the previous February—would capture the recruiting national championship in five of the six next seasons, according to Rivals.com.

It also confirmed that the Bowden era was nearing its end. But a beginning was coming—for Clemson and for Dabo.

CHAPTER 6

THE HEAD COACH

Early in the morning of October 13, 2008—a Monday—Clemson athletic director Terry Don Phillips met with Tommy Bowden in his office. The previous Thursday night, in front of a national audience on ESPN, Clemson had lost 12–7 to Wake Forest, dropping the Tigers' record to 3-3 overall and 1-2 in conference play. The goal of Clemson winning its first ACC championship in nearly two decades was now officially dead. If there had been an award for Most Disappointing Team in the Nation at the midway point of the 2008 season, the Tigers would have won in a landslide.

Phillips intended this 6:00 a.m. meeting to be a midseason review of the football team's performance and include a frank, heart-to-heart discussion with Bowden about what needed to change. At the time, Virginia Tech was the class of the ACC and Boston College and Wake Forest were routinely finishing ahead of Clemson in the Atlantic Division. The program was sputtering, but Phillips had no intention of firing Bowden at present. He simply wanted to know how Bowden, in his tenth season as head coach, was going to fix his team.

Questions surrounding what happened next remain up for debate—Did Phillips insist that Bowden resign at the end of the season? Was Bowden the first one to suggest he leave the program?—but what is clear is that Bowden told his boss, "Well, why don't we just make a change now?...If I'm the reason we're not having success, I need to remove myself now."

"There wasn't a gun to [Coach Bowden's] head," Phillips later said. "He put it on the table for the sake of the program. I agreed."

After accepting Bowden's resignation, the two men discussed who should take over the program for the remaining seven weeks of the season. "I myself would recommend Dabo," Bowden said. Phillips leaned back in his seat, quiet, deep in thought for what seemed like minutes to Bowden. It was as if he hadn't considered Dabo as an option, and he needed a moment to assess the recommendation. But Phillips wasn't as shocked as he may have appeared: He'd been paying close attention to Dabo ever since Bill D'Andrea had told him five years earlier about the unique skill set of the newly hired wide receivers coach from Alabama.

At about 10:30 a.m., Dabo—dressed in sweatpants and sweatshirt—and the rest of the assistants were told to gather in the staff meeting room. Once seated, Bowden strode in and told them that he had stepped down. He left and Phillips walked in, raised his hand to hush the room, and looked directly at Dabo. "Dabo, you're in charge," Phillips said. "You call all the shots. I need to see you in my office in five minutes."

The coaches sat in stunned silence, eyeing their new interim boss. Dabo rose from his chair and told the assistants that he'd talk to all of them after he spoke with Phillips. He then left the room. Before going to see Phillips, though, he did what he often did when facing a dilemma:

He called his wife.

THAT MORNING BEGAN AS usual for Kathleen. Her youngest son, Clay, wasn't feeling well. She had made breakfast for Will, now ten, and Drew, eight. After they ate and gathered their backpacks, she drove them to school and took Clay to the doctor's office, where he received medicine.

She returned home with Clay and tucked him under a blanket on the living room couch. She then started to cook a meal when her cell phone rang. "What are you doing?" Dabo asked.

"I'm making your chili," she replied, referring to one of Dabo's favorite foods.

Without saying okay or thanks, Dabo blurted, "Kat, Tommy is gone and I'm the head coach."

"What?" Kathleen replied.

She then asked Dabo a bunch of questions, rapid-fire, like: What is going to happen to us? Will we have to move? But then Dabo interrupted and said, "Baby, please pray for me because I have a lot of tough decisions right now."

Kathleen eventually called Linda Bowden, Tommy's wife.

She told her how sorry she was for what had happened and that their family loved them. But Linda assured her that they would be fine and that, in some ways, it was a relief that it was finally over. Linda said, "We're okay. And I'm so happy for y'all. Dabo is going to do a great job and we are fine."

AS DABO NEARED THE athletic director's office on the mid-autumn October morning, he knew that the odds of remaining at Clemson as the head coach for the long-term were slim to none. After all, of the previous twenty-nine coaches in major college football that held the job title of "interim head coach," not a single one was eventually promoted to the head coaching position at their school. Dabo had even more going against him: He wasn't even a coordinator, and the last time a position coach was named interim coach and then went on to become a head coach was...Well, no one at Clemson was really sure if it had ever happened.

Dabo had been at Alabama in 2000 when Mike DuBose and the staff found out about midway through the season that they were going to be fired, which they were after the final game on the schedule. It had been a gut-wrenching, emotional experience—one that neither Dabo nor Kathleen wanted to live through again. This sudden change of events meant that Dabo and his family would likely be moving to a new town after the season, which, in turn, meant their kids would be leaving their friends, their school, and all that was familiar to them. Their routines and their habits would have to change—always very stressful for young children.

Dabo entered Phillips's office carrying his notebook. Since joining Alabama's support staff back in 1993, he had kept a head-coaching notebook in preparation for this very moment. Throughout the years, he constantly added ideas, diagrams, principles, homilies, and philosophical thoughts about football and coaching that he might use if and when he became a head coach. But even Dabo was somewhat surprised that he was tapped for the interim position. There were two former head coaches on the staff—Brad Scott and Vic Koenning. Dabo had coached his son's Pee-Wee team when he worked in commercial real estate, but that was his only experience of being the man in charge. Even though Dabo had personally recruited thirty-eight of the eighty-five scholarship players on the 2008 team, he wasn't the obvious candidate to ascend to the top job for the remainder of the season.

Phillips and Dabo sat down, facing each other in Phillips's office. "I want you to know that I've watched you for five and a half years," the athletic director said. "And I want you to know that I think you're ready for this job."

Dabo listened intently. "Here's what I want you to do," Phillips continued. "For the next seven weeks, I don't want you to be the interim head coach. I want you to be the head coach. I want you to think like you're the head coach. I want you to do what you think you need to do to fix us. Do it, and you've got my full support. If you feel like you need to fire the whole staff, you've got my full support. I've watched in the community. I've watched your relationship with your players. I've watched how you coach on the field. I've watched you in recruiting. I've watched how you manage yourself, Dabo. I really believe you're what we need here. Now, I'm also going to tell you this: I'm going to hire the best coach for Clemson. I'm going to do a national search and I'm going to interview people. But what I want you to know is I would love to see you get this job."

Phillips also noticed that players frequently hung out in Dabo's office. They obviously enjoyed being in his orbit, and that illustrated to Phillips how much respect and admiration the players had for Dabo. There was just something magnetic about him, and now Phillips wanted that magnetism, his magic, to infuse the entire Clemson program—at least for the next seven weeks.

Dabo was taken aback. His sense of professionalism caused him to camouflage his utter delight at being given a legitimate chance to earn the permanent head coaching job, and he calmly thanked his athletic director and told him he was ready to accept the challenge. Minutes earlier he had genuinely believed that being handed the interim title was tantamount to a professional death sentence at Clemson, but now he felt that Phillips was sincerely rooting for him to succeed and earn the job.

Invigorated, Dabo went to work. He walked into a small break room, locked the door, and for nearly an hour poured his thoughts about what needed to be done onto several pieces of paper. He scribbled notes about practices, staff, fans, his team, and his recruiting plan. His meeting with Phillips had empowered Dabo. His fear of losing his job in seven weeks had turned into a hope of landing the job in seven weeks. Adrenaline surged through his veins as he vigorously wrote in his notebook. He felt ready because he knew he was prepared—the same way he was prepared when he was on the scout team at Alabama during his redshirt sophomore season and was told that he was getting a one-day trial with the varsity offense. He passed that test because he'd studied the Alabama offense like a coach, and that had given him the edge he needed. Now his years of note-taking on the art of coaching were about to pay off.

Dabo began implementing his plan, which started with a professional execution. He walked into the office of Rob Spence, the offensive coordinator, and told him that he would no longer be needed and fired him on the spot. Dabo hadn't agreed with Spence's play calling, not understanding why the team's best player, running back C.J. Spiller, had only touched the ball on offense 57 times through six games, an average of 9.5 times per game. Dabo was going to take over play-calling duties, and his top priority was going to be this: Put the ball into the hands of Spiller. (Over the last six games of the season, Spiller averaged 15.3 touches per game.)

Dabo then switched Billy Napier from tight ends coach to quarterbacks coach. He asked Napier to help him, game by game, with play calling and developing the offensive game plan. He then elevated graduate assistant Jeff Scott to wide receivers coach. Dabo considered Scott a rising star in the profession, and he wanted him to play a more prominent role in the program.

Late that afternoon, Dabo met with the team and informed them of what was happening. He asked the other coaches to leave the room; he wanted to speak directly to his players with no distractions, from his heart. "None of you owe me anything," Dabo told his players. "You came to this program to play for Tommy Bowden as head coach. If you want to leave, you still have your scholarship until the end of the year. But if you come to practice today, I expect you to be all in for the rest of the year. I am going to put everything I have into the job, and I expect you to do the same."

HEAD COACHING OPPORTUNITIES AT major programs like Clemson don't become available very often—since 1940, only eight different men have presided over the Tiger program. For five days, Dabo put in twenty hours at the office, assessing everything about Clemson football, from the depth chart to their practice routines to play calling to the players' nutrition to even how the team interacted with the fans. For the next game against Georgia Tech, which would be played at home, Dabo planned to institute the Tiger Walk—the now-famous 200-yard stroll through an ocean of fans about two hours before kickoff. (A reporter asked him what Bear Bryant would have thought of the Tiger Walk. Dabo quickly replied that Bear would have seen it as a "class" way of doing things.)

Dabo issued another decree: On road trips and on the bus to home games, everyone had to dress up. Warm-ups would no longer be allowed. Dabo wanted his players to don a coat and tie to reaffirm how important the day was—whenever you dress up, it is the mark of a special occasion—and to instill an element of class into the program that had been lacking. It was another small thing, but in Dabo's world, nothing is truly small.

DURING THE FIRST TWO days of being the interim head coach, Dabo didn't move into Bowden's old office in the McFadden Building. It just didn't feel right; he stayed in his small office that had a view of Littlejohn Coliseum and, in the distance, Death Valley. Dabo always had an open-door policy, which meant fans and media and players could come and go mostly as they pleased—as long as he wasn't in the middle of a project or some important task. He enjoyed talking ball and life with anyone, which was why he generally kept his office door open.

Then after the second day of practice as the interim head coach, Dabo loaded up his belongings in cardboard boxes and lugged them over to the corner office on the other side of the building. The office had a sliding glass door on one side that allowed the head coach to slip out and walk discreetly to his parking spot, a mere five feet away.

Early on Thursday morning—Day 4 on the job—Dabo drove to work in the dark. He hadn't slept more than a few fitful minutes Wednesday night, his mind occupied with all that he needed to do. He was also, for one of the few times in his life, filled with doubts. Phillips, the athletic director, had told Dabo to act like it was his job, that he wasn't just some placeholder, that he was the boss. Dabo had always projected confidence and optimism and hope, but now as he drove to work in the predawn on Thursday, so many questions attacked his

In spite of the problems in his home life, Dabo (number 81) was always on top of the world when he was with his high school football teammates. *Courtesy Pelham (Al.) High School*

Pictured here with fellow Pelham High student Shawn Glasscox, Dabo was named the school's "Most Talented" as a senior. *Courtesy Pelham (Al.) High School*

A class president and a member of the National Honors Society, Dabo was everybody's best friend at Pelham (Al.) High. *Courtesy Pelham (Al.) High School*

A multisport athlete in football, basketball, and baseball, Dabo (top row, fifth from left) earned multiple letters at Pelham High. *Courtesy Pelham (Al.) High School*

Dabo's former high-school sweetheart, Kathleen Swinney, has been by Dabo's side—and his most trusted confidante—even before they were married on July 9, 1994. *Icon Sports Wire via Getty Images*

An undersized, overachieving, walk-on wide receiver at Alabama, Dabo finished his Crimson Tide career with seven receptions for 81 yards. *Rodger Champion*

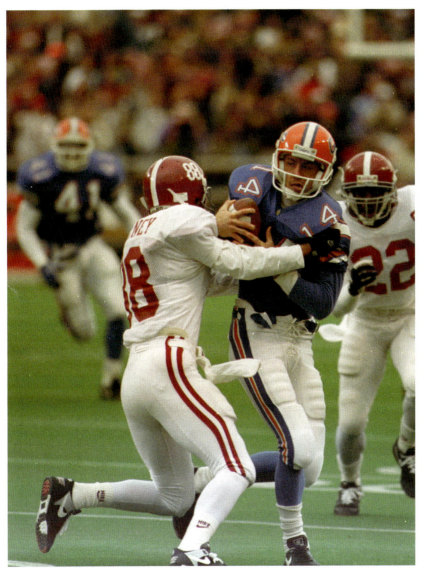

At Alabama, Dabo excelled on the Tide's special teams. Here he makes a critical tackle in the 1992 SEC Championship game against Florida. *Rodger Champion*

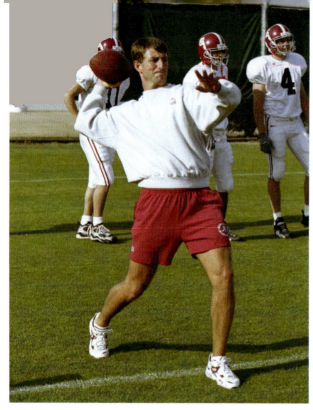

Dabo began his coaching career at Alabama in 1993 as a graduate assistant. A hands-on, show-by-example assistant, Dabo became the Crimson Tide's wide receivers coach in 1996— a position he would hold until he was let go in 2000. *Rodger Champion*

Hired by his former coach Gene Stallings, Dabo quickly impressed the veteran coaches on the Alabama staff with his agile football mind and his ability to cultivate close, meaningful, lasting relationships with his players. *Rodger Champion*

At Alabama and now at Clemson, Dabo has embraced the philosophy of his coaching hero Paul "Bear" Bryant: "Coach them hard and hug them harder later." *Rodger Champion*

Dabo is the first coach in Clemson history to run down The Hill, leading his players into Memorial Stadium at full sprint—a vivid illustration of his never-a-cloud-in-the-sky enthusiasm. *The State via Getty Images*

One of the most animated college football coaches in America, Dabo is constantly encouraging, clapping, and slapping high- and low-fives with his players on the sideline. As one former player puts it, "Coach Swinney is the most positive, uplifting person I've ever met—in or out of football." *Streeter Lecka via Getty Images*

Nick Saban and Dabo have faced each other four times in the College Football Playoffs. Swinney owns a vacation home in Florida only a few miles from Saban's getaway spot, and they have made friendly wagers over the years. So far, they are 2-2 against each other. *Rodger Champion*

thoughts: Was he up for the job? Was he ready? Could he win over the team? Could he win over the other coaches? More thoughts drifted through his mind as he steered his Ford Explorer along Highway 93 and then onto Perimeter Road.

Suddenly, the building was in view. The parking lot was empty. For the last half decade, he had always parked in a spot that faced away from the building. Now he was heading for his old spot when it hit him: The head coach didn't park where the other assistants did. He yanked on the wheel and headed toward the head coach's spot. *Man, this is real,* he thought.

Pulling into his spot, his low-beams illuminated the number of the parking space on the curb: 88—his jersey number at Alabama. He froze and then began sobbing. For the better part of his life, he believed in signs from above and interpreted them as God speaking directly to him. Still emotional, he called his wife, telling her, "You're not going to believe this." Minutes later, he walked through the sliding glass door.

That day, during a few free minutes, Dabo opened the top desk drawer in what had been Bowden's desk. Using a pen, he wrote his name on the bottom of the desk drawer. Over and over, he retraced the letters D-A-B-O, underlining them, imprinting the beginning of his legacy—whatever it would be—on Clemson football. No matter what happened in the future, as long as this desk was in the Tiger football offices, Dabo's name would have a place in the program. He made sure of that.

DABO IMPLEMENTED MORE CHANGES. He invited students to watch practice and even allowed some to participate, letting them attempt field goals, field punts, and boot punts against a live rush. More than a thousand students showed up. He brought the band to practice to enliven the atmosphere and increase school spirit. He welcomed faculty to practice; a horde of curious professors arrived and stood on the sideline. As an assistant coach, Dabo had come to believe that an invisible wall had been erected between the football team and the rest of the school, and he was doing everything in his power to sledgehammer that wall.

Dabo vowed to write back to any fan who wrote to him. In every one of those missives, he expressed his characteristic optimism, telling the fans that the distant horizons were filled with promise for Clemson football and that better days would soon arrive. He sold hope as astutely and consistently as a seasoned politician. He also tried to spend as much time as he could with reporters, engaging them, spinning colorful yarns about his past, currying their favor with his wit and charm. Tommy Bowden was a stoic man who didn't possess his dad's charisma. But that was one of Dabo's signature qualities, and both local and national reporters relished talking to this young interim head coach with the unique name. He was a quote machine, a writer's dream.

For years, dating back to his playing days at Alabama, reporters had asked Dabo about his family. And for years, he declined to go into the harsh details of his upbringing. But eventually he didn't want to run from his painful past any longer, so he opened up to several reporters, sparing no detail about the problems his family had faced when he was young. His father Ervil was upset at first—the anger didn't last long—but Dabo even encouraged his own family to share their own version of the events. It was liberating, unburdening, especially for his mother, Carol, who realized that only by talking about the past could she truly let go of it.

ON THE FRIDAY MORNING before the game against Georgia Tech—Day 5 on the job for Dabo—D'Andrea, the associate athletic director, called Dabo and asked him if he could take him to a meeting with the school's board of directors. By the tone of D'Andrea's voice, it sounded more like a demand than a request. "They just want to wish you well," D'Andrea said. "You might need to come."

Dabo entered the room with the board members. One said, "We're very committed here, but we just want to be great academically and athletically, like Georgia and Florida and Michigan."

Dabo later said that he tried to hold his tongue, but he just couldn't suppress the Alabama in him and so he spoke his mind. "Sir, I do not want to be disrespectful, but that is not my vision for Clemson at all," Dabo said. "I want for all those other schools to want to be like Clemson."

DABO TYPICALLY CARRIES A pen and index cards with him wherever he goes. As much as any coach in America, Dabo constantly writes notes, reminders, ideas, observations, and other football-related brainstorms that he thinks can help his program, even down to the names of motivational speakers who could inspire the team. Dabo had been doing this since his days as a player at Alabama, and most of the notebooks now are in boxes in his house, but some are in his office. He still flips through them, bringing back a flood of memories each time he reads his old words. And sometimes rereading those notes loosens long-forgotten details that prompt the blossoming of new ideas. Many will be tested on the practice field and some will be employed on the playing field.

Throughout his first week on the job, he lugged around his massive binder that served as his how-to guide for every aspect of the program. The binder contains every imaginable football subject—game day prep, recruiting, strength and conditioning, operations, tickets, maintenance, travel, administration, and so much more. There are also sections devoted to his philosophies and ideas on offense, defense, and special teams.

During his stretch as interim coach, Dabo and Kathleen often stayed up talking until the small hours of the morning. Dabo was hyper-focused on what he could do to bring the team closer together, to get the players to truly care for one another and create and foster a close-knit family. That was the culture he wanted to create at Clemson, and Kathleen would listen for hours about all the ideas Dabo had to make this happen. Kathleen had always been an excellent listener, and Dabo considered her to be his most valuable friend and teammate. For years he had bounced ideas off her, and now, deep into the night—night after night—he was doing it again, even at times wondering aloud if he was doing the right things.

Dabo sometimes revealed doubt to his spouse, but if there was one old truth in coaching, it was that a coach couldn't show weakness to anyone except his wife.

BY SATURDAY, HE WAS ready to roll. Minutes before kickoff against Georgia Tech, Dabo—on Day 6 of the job—led his players into Death Valley from the top of the steep hill behind the east end zone of Memorial Stadium. Dabo raised his arms skyward, pumping up the crowd, and kissed Howard's Rock. No coach in Clemson history had run down that hill leading his players onto the field—until Dabo. He had fretted about falling as he sprinted down the hill, but Dabo decided to go for it, go all in.

A shot from a cannon signaled Dabo's first step. He sprinted down the hill with a fresh-faced smile, looking like he was having the time of his life. He maintained his footing and then picked up the pace once he reached the field. Seeing the thirty-eight-year-old run as fast as he could prompted more than a few laughs in the crowd, but Dabo didn't care how corny or goofy he appeared. He continued to run past the cheerleaders, who were marching toward midfield as the Clemson band played the school's fight song. When he reached midfield, Dabo slowed and smiled again and yelled to the cheerleaders, "I beat you!" This run in the sun before the start of his first game as interim head coach was a telling moment—it showed everyone in attendance that Dabo was going do everything with joy and 100 percent effort.

Georgia Tech was 5-1, and the Yellow Jackets defeated

Clemson 21–17 to spoil Dabo's debut. The Tiger assistant coaches figured they needed to go 4-1 over the final five weeks of the season to have a real shot at keeping their jobs. The coaches knew it would be very difficult to defeat Florida State on the road on November 8, but Clemson had three extremely winnable games against Duke, Virginia, and South Carolina. This meant that the key game, in their view, would come against Boston College on November 1.

Clemson hadn't beaten the Eagles since 1958. The Tigers jumped to a 17–0 lead. But Boston College, playing at home, seized a 21–17 lead with a little more than eight minutes remaining in the fourth quarter. Dabo and his assistants knew what was on the line: If they lost this game, they would lose their jobs. After the Eagles had scored the touchdown to go up 4 points, offensive coordinator Brad Scott sat in the press box and realized that the remaining few minutes of the game could determine the next ten to fifteen years of his career. "Fortunately for us," Scott recalled, "we had somebody named C.J. Spiller."

Spiller—who Dabo had recruited and convinced to remain at Clemson when he considered transferring to Florida— returned the kickoff 64 yards. This set up the Tigers at the B.C. 15-yard line, and a few plays later Cullen Harper threw a 4-yard touchdown pass to Aaron Kelly. Clemson won the game 27–21. "You'd have thought we'd won the national championship that day," Swinney recalled. "It was just like, 'We believe and we've got a chance and we're on our way.' That was the wind in the sails that we needed."

Clemson lost to Florida State on the road but finished the season by beating Duke, Virginia, and rival South Carolina. Against the Gamecocks, Clemson jumped to a 24–0 lead and won 31–14. The team had finished the regular season 4-2 under their interim head coach, the record the assistants believed they needed to save their jobs and return for the 2009 season. Dabo didn't mention the importance of beating South Carolina in the locker room before the game; he didn't tell them what a win would probably mean. He didn't want to put added pressure on his players, but everyone associated with the program was aware of the significance of the game.

Against Gamecocks in the regular season finale, Dabo dug deep into his playbook. He ordered up a trick play called Cock-a-doodle-doo, resulting in a 50-yard touchdown throw from Cullen Harper to Jacoby Ford. As the final seconds wound down, 82,000 fans chanted and thundered "Dab-o Swin-ney! Dab-o Swin-ney!" Kathleen stood in the rain with the other wives and cheered and chanted along with everyone else. It was nine days after Dabo's birthday on November 20, and this had the feel of an overdue Happy Birthday serenade. When the final whistle blew, offensive guard Thomas Austin and a few other Clemson players hoisted Dabo to their shoulders and carried him to midfield. It was a special moment—for Dabo, for Kathleen, for anyone who cared about Clemson football.

"They thoroughly beat us," Steve Spurrier said. "We just got smashed. You can sugarcoat it all you want. That's a team that should have won the ACC, or could have won the ACC, I should say."

Dabo believed he had done enough to earn the job, but no one said anything to him after the game. He did, however, get a lot of winks and head nods and smiles. With all his heart, he believed he had beaten the odds and would become the next permanent head coach at Clemson.

D'ANDREA WAS Terry Don Phillips's closest confidante during the coaching search. The duo looked closely at Lane Kiffin (who had been out of football since being fired over the phone by Oakland Raiders owner Al Davis), Gary Patterson (the head coach at Texas Christian University), Bud Foster (the defensive coordinator at Virginia Tech), Will Muschamp (the defensive coordinator at Texas), and Brent Venables (the defensive coordinator at Oklahoma). Phillips employed a search consultant to assist him in his quest to find the right person for the job. Five coaches who were interviewed in person and a handful of others who were contacted all had experience as a head coach or as a coordinator. The only one who didn't was Dabo.

"That's the thing I wanted to make sure of, that we talked to people and did a legitimate search," Phillips later said. "I thought Dabo had a real shot, even though a lot of other people probably didn't, but I wanted to have other coaches to compare him to, and so much of it was the fit. What I kept coming back to was that Dabo was worth the gamble, if you want to call it a gamble, and I'd been around him enough to know that he was a great fit for Clemson."

And so on the day after Clemson defeated rival South

Carolina, Phillips offered Dabo the job. He accepted. The Tigers had won four of their last six games of the 2008 season, and Dabo had invigorated not just the team, but the entire fan base. What was more, he came cheap, accepting an annual salary of $800,000, which made him the lowest paid head coach in the ACC. A talking head on ESPN categorized the hire as a D+.

On Monday evening, December 1, 2008, Dabo was formally introduced as the Tigers' next head coach at a press conference. Dabo had so much to say—and so many stories to tell—that the presser ran long and preempted part of *The Bachelor* on the local ABC station. The show happened to be Bowden and his wife's favorite program, and Bowden later joked with Dabo about his motor mouth when he called to wish him well and express how proud he was of him.

"Had I not been prepared to be a head coach—as prepared as you can be—then this opportunity would have passed me by," Dabo said. "If your job is to go get the doughnuts, man, you bring the freshest doughnuts and the hottest coffee. And you do it in a way that everybody notices. 'That guy gets the best doughnuts in the history of the doughnut business.' And that's just how you have to do things."

At his introductory press conference, Dabo had to pause several times as he spoke, holding in his emotions. "There is only one reason that an ol' boy from Pelham, Alabama, is sitting in front of you today, and that's the grace of God," he said. "To be the head coach at Clemson, that doesn't just happen. The very first time I decided to park in the head coach's parking spot—because I was hesitant to do so—it was Thursday of that week. It was about 5:30 in the morning. It was pitch black. Wasn't anybody there. I pulled in that parking spot, and my lights hit the curb. I'd never parked in that spot before. I don't even know if it is the official head coach spot, but that's where he always parked. I pulled in that spot, and curb had No. 88. That was my college number, and it was just kind of like God saying, 'I got your back. Hang in there.' Things happen for a reason."

Not long after he was named Clemson's head coach, Dabo attended a luncheon banquet in Spartanburg, South Carolina. Along with a few other coaches, Dabo was slated to give a short speech. When he arrived at his seat, he went bug-eyed: Sitting next to him was Bill Curry, his old coach at Alabama, the one who gave him a chance to make the team as a walk-on. Curry was now the coach at Georgia State. Dabo didn't think Curry would even remember him, but Curry immediately recognized Dabo and told him he'd been watching him from afar with pride. After a few minutes, Curry said, "Dabo, you haven't asked for my advice, but I'm going to tell you three things."

Dabo quickly found a small of piece of paper and scooted his chair closer to the table, listening hard. First, Curry said, he needed to find a good financial advisor, because you never know when you're going to lose your job. Curry then emphasized that family was the most important thing, and he needed to always make time for his wife and kids, no matter if his team was winning or losing. Curry admitted he didn't always do this, and it was one of the most profound regrets of his life.

But it was Curry's final nugget of wisdom that really stuck with Dabo. He scribbled it down feverishly on the little white paper dated 12/19/08—a piece of paper that he would keep in his office for years. Dabo even circled the two words of advice that served as the fundamental lesson served up by his first college coach: "Be Dabo."

THAT OFF-SEASON IN college football, the Tennessee Volunteers hired Lane Kiffin, who had been fired in the middle of the previous season from the NFL's Oakland Raiders after stumbling to a 1-3 start. The Auburn Tigers hired Gene Chizik from Iowa State, who had a record of 5-19 in his previous two seasons. But of all the new hires at major schools in 2009, Dabo appeared to be the biggest risk—and the one most likely to fail because of his inexperience. When asked if he thought the school was taking a chance and gambling on him, he said, "No! If you are asking me, it's a pretty good bet. I don't mean that in an arrogant way. I'm confident in my abilities and always have been. I believe in myself."

Dabo ate his meals in the cafeteria of the football facility, not in his office or in a film room like many coaches did. He wanted to be as close to his players as possible, and he needed every player—from the starting quarterback to the fifth-string free safety—to consider him approachable. He believed that if he ate with his players, they would be more inclined to reach out to him when they had a problem or just wanted to shoot the bull. Fostering tight relationships with his players and coaches was paramount to Dabo, and he tried to work on those relationships every day on the job. He also had a noon basketball game that he played in; anyone was welcome as long as they didn't foul the head coach too hard.

But Dabo's long-term plan for Clemson extended far beyond building relationships and creating a family atmosphere. He may be the only coach in America with an undergraduate degree in commerce and business administration while also holding a master's degree in business administration. He talked to the higher-ups in the athletic department about the bell curve of a typical business: First there is birth, then growth, then decline, then eventually death. But Dabo repeatedly emphasized that the great businesses never plateau and never begin that downward spiral of decline. Instead, they figure out ways to consistently grow and evolve. This means you constantly have to reinvent yourself as a leader, reinvest in your product, reset how you do business, keep learning, keep innovating, keep growing, and—perhaps most important—keep changing.

Dabo only needed to direct his bosses' attention to Tuscaloosa, Alabama, to make his point. Nick Saban was constantly evolving. Most everyone in college football circles knew that Saban had a prototype for what he was looking for at each position, a height-weight-speed definition of the perfect player that Saban developed with Bill Belichick when Saban was the defensive coordinator for the Browns in 1991 and Belichick was the head coach. Unlike other teams that used scouts who had their own ideas and matrices of judging and measuring football skills, Belichick and Saban wanted to develop the team's own system for evaluating talent. So before the coaches looked at individual college players, the staff defined what they wanted in a player at each position. Debates ensued, ideas were exchanged, notes were taken, and before the draft, the Browns had identified the ideal height, weight, size, and speed for every position. At center, for example, the team determined that the desired size was 6'3", 280 pounds, with a 5.19-second 40-time. A player was then evaluated based on those ideal measurables. Other important factors at every position were also weighed, such as athletic ability, strength, playing speed, and character. But when assessing a player, he was always compared to the Browns' created prototype. And Saban learned never to look simply at players; rather he examined players in the context of the definitions of what the team wanted at each position.

At Alabama, Saban still used the concept of the prototype, but he tinkered with it every season based on how the game was evolving. For instance, he used to love big linebackers such as Rolando McClain (6'4", 255 pounds) and Dont'a Hightower (6'3", 260 pounds). But then in the early 2010s, spread offense proliferated throughout the nation. Suddenly, Saban's big, run-stuffing linebackers became liabilities in pass coverage. So what did Saban do? He changed the prototype of what he wanted at the middle linebacker position, seeking smaller, faster players who could cover in space.

Dabo was well aware that Saban was constantly evolving

and trying to stay ahead of the changing nature of how football was played. He knew that Saban and Alabama were the gold standard of the sport; if Clemson was ever going to roll with the Tide, Dabo needed to pay attention to the type of players Alabama was recruiting. Specifically, Dabo needed to know the prototype that Saban and his staff were employing at each position. What was more, Dabo believed that Clemson needed to at least match what the Crimson Tide was doing off the field in terms of their facilities and their vast academic support network for their players.

After Dabo became head coach, he frequently met with Terry Don Phillips. Dabo constantly requested more from his athletic director—more facilities, more support staff, more academic support—all of which cost money. When Phillips questioned the necessity of the requests, he'd ask Dabo, "Why?"

Dabo typically responded quickly and with concrete certainty every time: "Well, Alabama does it."

EVERY SUMMER DABO GATHERED his staff for a five-day retreat. He called it his "All In" meeting. The working document at the retreat is a six-inch-thick, white binder that contains pages and pages that detail every aspect of the Clemson football program. Dabo calls the manual the "All-In Book" and describes it as a "living, breathing" organism. The staff reads every page together as they create a specific plan for the upcoming season.

During the retreat, the coaches discuss their job descriptions and duties. They examine the depth chart with the diligence of crime scene investigators, determining with clear eyes the team's strengths and weaknesses. They review their philosophy on recruiting, taking time to discuss what type of player they are looking for at each position the way Saban and his staff do. They zero in on the recruits that they want the most, and talk about what kind of special attention they plan to give those recruits. Dabo also presents a calendar of his season—a day-by-day account of where he plans to be and what he plans to be doing.

About a third of the "All-In Book" reveals Dabo's philosophy on how to build character in young men and how to help them emotionally grow. Many of Dabo's favorite phrases are in this book: *serve a player's heart, not his talent; the little things lead to big things; iron sharpens iron.*

Dabo prides himself on not being a micromanager, on giving his coaches a wide berth to do their jobs—unless a situation spirals out of control and demands his attention. By staying out of the way as much as possible, that gives every staff member an increased sense of ownership and pride in what they do. And Dabo reminds everyone at these All-In meetings that he wants his coaches to know everyone else's job and their responsibilities, including the janitors and secretaries who work in the football facility. The word *family* is consistently used and emphasized.

EARLY IN HIS HEAD coaching career, Dabo did his best to balance his work life with his family life. He often met

Kathleen at 12:30 p.m. for a run around campus. If one of his boys had a game that conflicted with a meeting, he'd try to reschedule the meeting so he could be at the game. During the season, he hosted Family Night each Wednesday, one of Dabo's favorite weekly events. All of the coaches and their wives and children would come to the coach's offices on the fourth floor around 7:00 p.m. Dabo would "work the room," according to one former staffer, shaking hands, making small talk, posing for pictures, connecting with spouses, even kissing babies and tickling those in strollers. One observer noted that he'd never seen an individual love being around people more than Dabo.

BEFORE THE 2009 SEASON, Dabo and his staff traveled to Austin, Texas, to visit Mack Brown and his Texas Longhorn coaches. Gene Stallings was close to Brown and so was Woody McCorvey, a former Alabama assistant whom Dabo had hired as the program's athletic director of football administration. McCorvey set up the visit.

Led by quarterback Colt McCoy, Texas would play in the national championship that season, where they fell to the Crimson Tide 37–21. During this visit, which was more of a fact-finding mission, Dabo kept asking Brown and the Texas staff members the same question: How do you build a winning program? By the time the Clemson staff was flying back to South Carolina, Dabo had filled several notebooks with ideas.

At the early stage of Dabo's head coaching career, McCorvey

was his most trusted confidant, his top lieutenant, his consigliore. Dabo called him his "national security advisor," but it was hard to put into words just how valuable McCorvey was to Dabo. McCorvey had been Alabama's wide receivers coach from 1990 to 1997, and he was one of Dabo's first college coaches. McCorvey had admired the scrappy, never-give-up walk-on from the first day he met him, and when McCorvey became Alabama's first African American offensive coordinator in 1996, he lobbied Stallings to elevate Dabo from graduate assistant to wide receivers coach, which Stallings did. McCorvey gave Dabo a chance—and Dabo never forgets people who show faith in him.

When Dabo was hired at Clemson, one of the first people he called was McCorvey. "Woody, I need you to come be by my side," Dabo said. "I don't want you to come coach a position. I want you to help me coach life. I want you to help me run the program." Dabo went on to explain that he wanted McCorvey to be his big-picture thinker. Dabo trusted McCorvey as much as he trusted his wife, and he loved him like a father. There wasn't anyone else he wanted for this job.

McCorvey was hesitant—he was the offensive coordinator at Mississippi State at the time and he wasn't sure he wanted to leave coaching—but Dabo was persistent, telling him he needed him, putting on his full sales pitch. McCorvey eventually said he'd try it for a year and then reevaluate. But it didn't take long before McCorvey—at the urging of Dabo—started touching every aspect of Clemson's program. At different points he oversaw the budget, met regularly with the athletic director, interacted with the academic support staff, and worked with the players' council. He was sensitively attuned to the possibility of rifts between players, between coaches, and between players and coaches—and he'd take immediate steps to resolve them. McCorvey often said that it was his job to make sure that Dabo was never surprised by anything that reached his office or came across his desk.

The river of trust between Dabo and McCorvey ran deep. Both were raised in small rural towns on Highway 31 in Alabama— Dabo in Pelham and McCorvey in Atmore, three hours north of Pelham. Like Dabo, McCorvey didn't grow up rich, but he made the best he could of his own situation. And like Dabo, he is now a member of the Alabama sports Hall of Fame. To this day, Dabo credits McCorvey with shaping his football life.

"Highway 31 and the little pigskin brought these two men together and he's been like a best friend," Dabo said of Mc-Corvey years after he had hired him. "He's been like a father to me in my life."

THE R.M. COOPER LIBRARY at Clemson owns a Bible that once belonged to Clemson cadet B.H. Lawrence, who was a member of the class of 1903. He played football at Clemson for John Heisman, the Tigers' football coach from 1900 to 1903, whose name is now on a trophy coveted by every kid who has ever played a down of Pee-Wee football. In the back of the Bible, which has become known as the "Heisman Bible," Lawrence wrote plays and advice that his head coach had given his players.

In 1900—or 108 BD (Before Dabo)—Heisman led Clemson

to its first undefeated season (6-0) and its first conference championship. That fall the Tigers outscored their opponents 222–10 and beat Alabama and Georgia for the first time in school history. Eighty-two years later, coach Danny Ford guided Clemson to its first national championship, defeating Nebraska in the 1982 Orange Bowl 22–15 behind the stellar play of MVP quarterback Homer Jordan and wide receiver Perry Tuttle. Before Dabo arrived, Ford and Heisman were the school's most well-known and well-respected coaches.

In 1896, Walter Merritt Riggs—now know as the "Father of Clemson Football"—first introduced football to Clemson. Riggs had learned the game at Alabama's Agricultural and Mechanical College (now Auburn University), and it's no coincidence that Clemson shares its nickname with Riggs's former school. Using old orange-and-navy-blue uniforms that he brought from Auburn—after a few washboard scrubbings, the navy-blue on the jerseys faded into a purplish color— Riggs coached the Tigers to a 2-1 record in their inaugural year. But it was Heisman and his spectacular 1900 season that announced Clemson as a national force in college football.

Cadet Lawrence included Coach Heisman's 14 Do's and Don'ts in Football in his bible, which young Lawrence would study during chapel. The last two pieces of advice in the "Heisman Bible" summed up whether Dabo Swinney would make it as Clemson's coach. They read:

DO: WIN
DON'T: LOSE

CHAPTER 7

THE BUILDING OF DABO'S DYNASTY

After he was elevated to permanent head coach on December 1, 2008, one of Dabo's top priorities was to find his quarterback of the future. Three months into his new job, he sat in the kitchen of Tajh Boyd, one of the most accomplished quarterbacks in the history of high school football in the state of Virginia. As a starter at Phoebus High in Hampton, Virginia, the dual-threat quarterback went 43-2 and guided his team to two state championships. He then was named the co-MVP of the 2009 U.S. Army All-American Bowl after he completed seven of nine passes for 179 yards and three touchdowns.

Dabo knew Boyd wouldn't be an easy get. The coveted quarterback had committed to West Virginia in 2008, but then flipped his commitment to Tennessee. Then the Vols' coach Phillip Fulmer was replaced by Lane Kiffin, who preferred pro-style quarterbacks, not signal-callers such as Boyd who could make plays with both his arms and his feet. The Kiffin hire prompted Boyd to again terminate his commitment. The door was now open for Dabo, but the chances of landing Boyd were slim: Ohio State and Oregon were his top choices. But this didn't deter Dabo, who admired Boyd's toughness and his dedication to his teammates. In his senior year at Phoebus High, he played with a torn knee ligament and still threw twenty-three touchdown passes.

On the day of his visit to Boyd's home, Dabo spotted Ohio State coach Jim Tressel and Oregon coach Mike Belotti near the house awaiting their turn to talk with Boyd. Seeing those "enemy" coaches strengthened Dabo's resolve to sway Boyd and prove that he could out-recruit—and basically outsell—two of the nation's top coaches. Dabo spoke to Boyd at the kitchen table and detailed his vision for him and Clemson football, painting a vivid word picture of what they could do together in Death Valley, how they would awaken the echoes of past greatness at the school. "Tajh, here's the plan," Dabo said. "If you'll believe in me, we'll change Clemson. We'll change it. It's not going to be easy. We've got work to do, but we will change Clemson."

The former shopping center leasing agent did it again: Boyd committed to Clemson, further cementing Dabo's status in college football circles as one of the country's most formidable recruiters. After redshirting in 2009, Boyd—the centerpiece of Dabo's first recruiting class—became the starter in 2011, his sophomore season. Boyd would finish his career with school records for passing yards (11,904) and passing touchdowns

(107) and would be tied for most wins as a starting quarterback (32) with Rodney Williams and Deshaun Watson.

Boyd kick-started Dabo's recruiting machine as Clemson's head coach. He reeled in five straight top 20 ranked recruiting classes (including top 10 classes in 2011 and 2012), which made Clemson just one of five teams in the nation with five straight ESPN Top 20 classes. As the river of talent flowed onto campus, the Tigers inched closer to national prominence. During Boyd's career as a starter, Clemson knocked off the likes of Ohio State, Louisiana State University, Georgia, Florida State, and Auburn.

Game by game, victory by victory, a new culture—Dabo's culture—was taking root in Clemson.

IN MARCH 2009, CLEMSON held a Pro Day for running back C.J. Spiller, the most important recruit that Dabo brought to the school when he was an assistant coach. NFL scouts flocked to Clemson to scrutinize the athletic prowess of Spiller. On the morning of his Pro Day, the skies opened over Death Valley and rain poured down. Clemson didn't have an indoor practice facility; Spiller had to showcase his skills on the Tigers' wet outdoor turf field.

Dabo watched from under an umbrella alongside John Fox, then the coach of the Carolina Panthers. As raindrops pounded on his star player—the player who may have single-handedly delivered him the permanent coaching job at Clemson with his long kickoff return late in the game against Boston College the previous fall—Dabo was overwhelmed with embarrassment. He believed that both he and the school had failed Spiller.

Dabo walked back to his office and then spoke to the media. "I'm embarrassed," he said. "I'm embarrassed that we didn't have better for C.J. Spiller." He then talked to Phillips, the athletic director, and told him, "We need an indoor facility. This is an embarrassment. We're better than this. Best is the standard."

Not long after this talk, Phillips started a fundraising campaign to build a $10 million, eighty-thousand-square-foot indoor practice facility. It opened in January 2013 and featured a full-sized, synthetic turf football field, four play clocks, a scoreboard, and a video board the same size as the one in Memorial Stadium. Like Saban at Alabama, Dabo was wielding more and more power at Clemson, his requests of his athletic director usually green-lit. Naturally, this had been a key component of Dabo's plan from the moment he was named head coach.

THE BUILDING BLOCKS FOR a dynasty were starting to fall into place—the elite recruiting classes, the facilities—but the early years weren't always filled with sunshine. In Dabo's second full season, 2010, the Tigers lost the final game of the regular season at home to South Carolina, dropping their record to 6-6. After his postgame press conference, Dabo spotted Kathleen in a hallway. Visibly upset, she said that his boss, Terry Don Phillips, was in his office and wanted to see him. Dabo figured he was about to be fired. He thought to himself,

God never says oops. I did the best I could and I'm thankful for the opportunity.

Dabo approached the office. The door was barely cracked open and the overhead lights were off. Phillips sat alone on a couch under the glow of a single lamp. "Sit down," Phillips said.

Dabo took a seat. "Dabo, I'm going to tell you something," Phillips said. "I know you're disappointed. I know it's a tough time. There's going to be negativity. There's going to be some criticism. There's going to be this and that, but here's what I want you to know—I'm more confident right now, at this moment, that you're the guy for this job, that you're going to be successful, than I was before I hired you. That's all I got to say. If you need me, you call me."

A few weeks later, the Tigers lost to South Florida in the Meineke Car Care Bowl in Charlotte. There were large swaths of empty seats—an indication that apathy among Clemson football fans was growing, not declining—and the Tigers finished the season 6-7, the team's first losing record in twelve years. Dabo knew he likely wouldn't survive another year if it was anything like the one he had just experienced. Feeling like he had nothing to lose, he did what all the good coaches do when things aren't going well: He took risks and made changes.

The biggest risk was the hiring of offensive coordinator Chad Morris—a longtime high school coach—even though Morris had only one year of college experience at Tulsa. But under Morris's guidance as Tulsa's coordinator, the Golden Hurricanes' offense was one of the most prolific in the nation, increasing its total offense by 23.3 percent from the previous year by averaging 505.6 yards per game in 2010. Their scoring average jumped 41.5 percent (the offense averaged 41.4 points per game) and they doubled their win total from five to 10.

Morris was pure Lone Star, his accent as thick as Texas crude. He grew up in Edgewood, Texas, attended Texas A&M, and spent sixteen years coaching high school football in Texas, where his teams won three state titles and appeared in six championship games. His success at Tulsa had caught Dabo's eye, but Dabo had never met Morris. Dabo called Gus Malzahn—then the offensive coordinator at Auburn who was close to Morris—and quizzed him about Morris. Dabo was digging and learning about not just Morris's football mind, but also about his character and his values.

"I didn't know Chad, and obviously [Gus] gave me some confirmation on who he was as a person," Dabo said. "I was more interested in that. There are a lot of good coaches out there. I always tell people, 'Good coaches are a dime a dozen.' Good coaches who are good people, good husbands, good fathers, who love their players and are passionate about doing things in a way that I believe is important, that pool gets real small."

Dabo convinced the school to pay Morris an annual salary of $1.3 million, a staggering sum for a man one year removed from coaching high school ball. Then on January 13, 2011, Dabo introduced Morris as his new offensive coordinator at a press conference. "What can fans expect to see out of this offense?" a reporter asked.

Morris grinned, as if he knew a secret and was dying to share it. "Well, we've got several hours here, so let's get comfortable." Then Morris spelled out a vision of a no-huddle, fast-paced spread that emphasized running the ball. He wanted to be physical at the point of attack on the line of scrimmage while opening wide lanes for the counter, zone, power runs, and toss sweeps. If the running game was humming, Morris emphasized that play action would create chances for long strikes downfield.

"There are a lot of teams in this country that are going to spread the field from sideline to sideline, but there are very few teams that try to put stress on a defense going vertical," Morris said. He added, "You get good at what you do. You don't trick people. You line up, and you play your style of football."

BEFORE THE SEASON OPENER against Auburn in 2012 Dabo made a hard decision: He suspended wide receiver Sammy Watkins—who had been voted the ACC's preseason player of the year weeks earlier—for the first two games of the season. Watkins had been pulled over on a traffic stop on May 4, 2012, and police found in his possession marijuana and two pills for which he didn't have a prescription. Watkins deserved to be suspended, but when Dabo meted out the punishment, even cynical reporters were surprised that he would sit his star player for the important, nationally televised game against Auburn. Coaches often suspended key players for games against powder-puff programs or didn't remove them from the lineup at all, preferring to handle the matter of discipline "internally." But not Dabo. He felt strongly that Watkins needed to be taught a harsh life lesson about incorrect actions having consequences.

This shattered the perception that Dabo had the softest heart in the sport. Ever since he was a kid, he'd always believed in accountability and being held responsible for your behavior. He'd never had much sympathy when he saw "people throwing their lives away and [saw] their lives' obstacles as excuses to fail." When he uttered words like these, it was as if he was speaking about his father.

Dabo's tough love extended to his own family. His brother Tripp sank so far into alcoholism and social despair that he ended up homeless in Atlanta. Dabo said for "20 something years he just threw his life away." But then his brother finally called him and asked for help. Dabo told his brother he would extend his hand and try to uplift him, but it had to be on Dabo's terms. Tripp accepted the offer and Dabo paid for Tripp's stint in a rehab center.

Yet Tripp's problems weren't solved then. A few years later, he was arrested in Panama City Beach, Florida, on an aggravated stalking charge for, among other things, sending his estranged wife nude pictures of herself and leaving threatening voice mail messages. "There's consequences for your actions," Dabo told reporters. "If you don't do the right thing, you suffer the consequences. I'm no different from anybody else, my family's no different than anybody else...One thing I learned a long time ago is you can't change people. People have to want to change and do the right things. Unfortunately, he's had a long history of not doing the right things. But I love him; he's my brother. There's nothing I can do about it and I done everything I can to be a good brother help him but that's his life and those are decisions that he's made."

IN OCTOBER 2011–TEN months after he introduced Chad Morris as his offensive coordinator—Dabo spoke to a reunion of the 1981 Tiger team. On a Friday night before Clemson played North Carolina, Dabo started talking about Steve Jobs. "The Apple guy?" someone asked. Yes, Dabo said.

"I heard a quote about him from President Obama," Dabo said. "This was a man who was brave enough to think differently." Dabo said that their 1981 national-title winning team was brave enough to think differently, and they ended up in the history books. He went on and on about how they were brave enough to think differently by taking care of each other—and how they've been taking care of each other ever since their playing days were over. He was talking about love—the love that Dabo had felt (and still felt) for his team-mates on the 1992 Alabama team that had won the national championship. "I understand the bond you have," Dabo said. Now, Dabo said, he was trying to get his own players to feel that love and forge that bond. The next day, Clemson beat the Tar Heels 59–38.

By season's end, with Morris's offense fully installed and with Morris calling the plays, the Tiger offense had shattered several school records. Clemson won its first ACC championship in twenty years. The gutsy hire had paid off—and, more and more, the players were starting to feel that love for each other. They were—according to multiple players on that team—starting to truly believe in Dabo.

THE SECOND KEY HIRE of Dabo's regime took place in January 2012. The Tiger defense had been bludgeoned by West Virginia in the Orange Bowl at the conclusion of the 2011 season, losing 70–33. In the 109-year history of bowl games, it had been a historically inept performance, as the Clemson defense set bowl game records for surrendering the most points in a quarter (35), a half (49), and a game (70). After the bloodbath was over, Dabo fired defensive coordinator Kevin Steele, who would later become an excellent coordinator in the SEC but struggled at Clemson handling the attack of spread offenses. Within a week of the Orange Bowl blowout, Dabo started his search for Steele's replacement.

Dabo had a coach in mind when, on a Thursday afternoon in January, Terry Don Phillips handed him a piece of paper that had the cell phone number of Oklahoma's co-defensive coordinator Brent Venables on it. "Hey look, do with [Brent's number] what you want," Phillips told Dabo. "But Brent reached out to me and said he'd be interested in talking to you if you are interested. He said he likes watching y'all every time you're on TV."

Dabo, who had never met Venables, was skeptical. "I'm kind of on a different path here. But I'll give him a call. I appreciate that."

At home that night, Dabo told his wife that he was going to make a quick call to Venables. He said it wouldn't last long. The two talked from about 9:00 p.m. to midnight on topics from football to family to faith—three hours that would prove monumental to the growth of Clemson football.

At Dabo's invitation, Venables and his wife flew to Clemson. Dabo met the couple as they checked into the Martin Inn, a quaint hotel on Madren Center Drive. The next day, Dabo gave them a personal tour around town, touting Clemson's small town feel, the culture of family that he had sowed, and the importance of faith that pervaded the program. The Venables fell in love with the place. But Dabo was adamant about one thing: If Venables wanted the job, he couldn't bring in his own staff.

"No, you don't get to bring nobody," Dabo said. "I hire everybody. Nobody hires anybody here except me. We've got to understand that right out of the gate. And you'll thank me later. Because these are all great men and great coaches."

From afar, Venables had been watching Dabo. Even though he had great affection for his own head coach Bob Stoops—he considered him to be like a brother—there was something about Dabo that intrigued Venables. He admired how he interacted with his players on the sideline, showing obvious affection and love for them. To Venables, Dabo seemed 100 percent genuine and authentic. His perception of Dabo was confirmed during his visit to Clemson. He accepted the job and Dabo now had his new defensive coordinator—one who had experience in defending spread offenses in the Big 12.

For the next decade, Venables would be by Dabo's side and establish himself as one of the top defensive minds in college football, winning the Broyles Award in 2016 for being the nation's top assistant coach.

Dabo now had two critical pieces in his program building in place—a talented offensive coordinator and a gifted defensive coordinator. To propel his program to the next level, though, he wanted one more thing:

A football facility that would be the envy of every coach in the nation, including the one in Tuscaloosa, a sprawling complex, a towering gridiron cathedral that would propel Clemson to the forefront of the facility arms race.

THE 70-33 ORANGE BOWL thrashing reinforced a negative national perception of Clemson: The Tigers didn't play well in big games. That dated to 2008, when an up-and-coming Alabama team demolished Clemson 34–10 in the season opener in Atlanta. In 2014, the Tigers were considered a legitimate national title contender but fell to Florida State in overtime 23–17, despite the absence of the Seminoles' future Heisman-winning quarterback, Jameis Winston, who sat out due to a one-game suspension. The loss popularized the term *Clemsoning*, which the Urban Dictionary defined as "the act of delivering an inexplicably disappointing performance, usually within the context of a college football season. The *Washington Post* headline over a story about the game the following morning said it all: "Against Florida State, Clemson's 'Clemsoning' Was the Most 'Clemsoning' Clemson Ever Clemsoned."

Dabo despised the derisive term. When a reporter asked him about it in 2015 when his team was 5-0 and had just beaten Georgia Tech 43–24, he erupted—a very rare reaction—in front of the gathered media, delving into a fifty-one-second diatribe on how that term needed to be eradicated. "I'm sick of it," he said. "I don't even know why [you] bring up the dagum word? How about these other teams who lose to un-ranked teams all the time? We ain't lost to anyone unranked since 2011, but I have to come to a press conference in 2015 and get asked that. And that's all media bull crap."

If there was any way to light Dabo's fuse, just say "Clem-soning," especially at a press conference. He considered the word a denigration of the honor and values of his program. And he knew there was but one way to make the derogative expression go away:

Consistently win big games.

SHORTLY AFTER DAN RADAKOVICH was hired as Clemson's new athletic director on October 29, 2012—Terry Don Phillips retired earlier that year—he asked Dabo what resources he needed to transform Clemson into a national power, one that could consistently compete for national championships. Dabo grabbed a pen and sketched a grand football facility. "Well, we're going to need some money," Radakovich told his coach.

Dabo and Radakovich put together an ambitious fund-raising plan. It called for elite donors to give $2.5 million each to the massive project, even though no one in the history of

Clemson athletics had ever made a single donation of that amount. Yet now the Tiger coach and athletic director planned to ask several boosters with deep pockets to dig deeper than ever. The key, Radakovich told Dabo, was winning over Leon J. Hendrix Jr., one of the most influential members of the board of trustees. But it wouldn't be easy to convince Hendrix to free up funds from his bank account. He had just given several hundred thousand dollars to assist the building of a new locker room, and Hendrix believed that was enough; he had done his part, end of story. Plus, Hendrix didn't think the team needed a sparkling new complex because it had recently moved into the renovated WestZone facility. Hendrix's wife, Pam, also shared that sentiment. It would be a tough sell, but if Dabo could convince Hendrix to stroke a check for $2.5 million, Radakovich believed others would follow.

Dabo went to work. In June 2012, he flew on a private jet to the South Carolina Lowcountry and met with Hendrix and his wife at their house on Kiawah Island, off the Atlantic coast, twenty-five miles southwest of Charleston. Dabo knocked on the door and shook the hand of Hendrix, a successful businessman who had spent ten years being in charge of Remington Arms, a gun manufacturer. Hendrix had been the Clemson student body president in 1963 and earned a bachelor's degree and attended graduate school there. Each of his four children also went to Clemson, and he loved Tiger football nearly as much as he loved his kids.

Hendrix guided Dabo to the back porch, where the two sat down on chairs and looked out over the roiling deep blue Atlantic. Dabo quickly took command. He revealed his vision for the football Shangri-La he wanted to build, a 140,000-square-foot facility that would require $35.5 million in donations (and cost a total of $55 million) and feature a movie theater, bowling lanes, laser tag, volleyball courts, and a barber shop, among other amenities. It will be, Dabo emphasized, the ultimate recruiting tool and a place that will provide so much enjoyment and homelike comfort to players that they won't want to leave Clemson.

During their conversation, Hendrix's wife brought out pizza. At one point Dabo asked Hendrix if he saw Clemson win its only national title back in 1981.

"Hell yes," Hendrix said.

"Do you ever want to win another one?" Dabo asked.

"Hell yes, I do!" Hendrix said.

"Well," Dabo said, jabbing himself in the chest with his forefinger, "I'm your best hope." Dabo then paused, locked his eyes on Hendrix, and said, "And you're my best hope."

Hendrix agreed to give Dabo the $2.5 million. As Dabo drove away, Pam looked to her husband and asked, "Do you think we gave them enough?"

AT THE NOVEMBER 2015 groundbreaking ceremony for the football facility, Dabo addressed the crowd, his eyes misty and his voice halting yet strong. "When I got this job, everybody talked about the good old days," he said. "Everybody walks around like the best is behind us. I'm telling you, the best is yet to come. This is the good old days. This is the best of times. And what this facility does, what this facility means when we stick a shovel in the ground, what we're saying is the best is yet to come."

During the entire fundraising process, Dabo never lost sight of the big picture. He knew how to tap into donors' passions and get them to do something they didn't necessarily want to do—the surest sign of a gifted salesman. He zeroed in on the key players, knowing that if he won them over, others would follow. It was yet another lesson in the course called Dabo's Leadership.

AT THE START OF Tommy Bowden's final season at Clemson in 2008, he had a staff of nine assistants, two graduate assistants, a pair of video graduate assistants, and two football administrators. The entire payroll for the miniscule support staff—positions such as analysts and director of player personnel—was just short of $290,000. Six years later, with Dabo in the throes of his empire building, the payroll for the support staff of eighteen had swelled to $1.47 million.

Dabo and his growing staff were constantly trying to figure out why certain recruits opted not to come to Clemson. In 2013, for example, the Tigers failed to land Top 25 recruits Montravius Adams (a future third-round pick by the Packers) and Carl Lawson (a future fourth-round pick by the Bengals), both defensive linemen. When Clemson coaches asked them why they spurned the Tigers, both players noted that Auburn had superior housing for its college football players. The next year the Clemson staff visited Auburn to share ideas and philosophies and coaching techniques—a common practice among coaching staffs. On a lunch break, Jeff Scott, who was then Clemson's wide receivers coach, wandered over to the apartments where Auburn players lived and asked a resident if he could snap a few photos. He did and then showed them to Dabo. About a month later, Clemson began renovating player housing, undertaking multiple $1 million makeovers to make living more comfortable for the players—and more enticing for recruits. The construction was paid for by the money the football program generated for the school; from 2012 to 2017, Clemson football brought in at least $43 million each season.

In the brick-by-brick assembly of his program, Dabo tried to do everything with his players in mind. Dabo has described Clemson as a "relationship-driven program." It's difficult for him to enjoy meaningful individual relationships with every one of his hundred players or so, but Dabo has set up a unique way to try to connect to everyone—including his dozens of assistants and support staffers—as best he can. On Mondays, he meets with a leadership group. Called the Swinney Council, it features senior leaders and typically a few underclassmen. On Tuesdays a group of assistants and staffers Dabo calls the Swinney Huddle gets together. Dabo isn't present, but the group produces a written report on the topics that were broached. Plus, Dabo hangs around the players as much as possible in the locker room and cafeteria, and at Family Night functions, trying to be as accessible as any coach in America.

"He can just talk and talk forever," said Hunter Renfrow, a wide receiver who arrived at Clemson in 2014. "Every single day, we're getting hammered with messages about how we can become better people, how we can become better football players. He can go on for hours sometimes, just because it means so much to him."

Dabo consistently repeats phrases, messages, and stories over and over. This is by design and is a lesson he learned from his former coach at Alabama, Gene Stallings. "When you say it enough so your players repeat it," Dabo said, "that's when you know they're getting it."

One message Dabo constantly hammers is that players need to clean up after themselves, a dictum he lives by as well. Like most college teams, Clemson typically rents out a movie theater the night before a game. Once the movie is over, a staffer brings out a leaf blower. Dabo is proud of the fact that no movie theater manager has ever complained about a single kernel of popcorn being left on the floor after Clemson's movie nights.

In Dabo's world, the little things always mean a lot.

THE RISE OF CLEMSON under Dabo wasn't swift. He went 9-5 in his first full season in 2009, capped by a 21–13 win over Kentucky in the Music City Bowl and a No. 24 ranking in the final AP poll. That was followed by a 6-7 campaign in 2010. But then, as the level of the program's recruiting increased and the on-campus facilities started to be built, Dabo led the Tigers to four consecutive ten-win seasons between 2011 and

2014; Clemson was one of only four schools in the country to achieve that feat over that span. Clemson was now ready to compete and beat the blue bloods of college football, which was vividly displayed when the Tigers throttled Oklahoma 40–6 in the Russell Athletic Bowl on December 29, 2014, in Orlando, Florida. But the biggest story to come out of Clemson that season was the emergence of a freshman quarterback named Deshaun Watson, a player who would soon become one of the most important of the Dabo Swinney era at Clemson.

Only months into his job as the Tigers' offensive coordinator in 2011, Chad Morris drove eighty miles to Gainesville, Georgia, to watch a high school freshman play basketball. Morris knew all about this young athlete who was also on the football team. The previous fall, Deshaun Watson had started for Gainesville High, finishing the season with 2,088 passing yards, 569 rushing yards, and 22 touchdowns. The entire Clemson staff had been entranced by Watson's play, his grace on the field, the power of his arm, and his ability to lead his team even as a freshman. He also was a young man of faith.

Morris developed a relationship with Watson. He repeatedly made the eighty-mile drive from his office to visit with the quarterback, forging a bond with him. The summer before his sophomore year, Morris convinced Watson to come to a football camp at Clemson so he could throw in front of Dabo. Once on campus, it didn't take long for Dabo to formally offer Watson a scholarship, explaining to Watson he would be a perfect fit in the new up-tempo, spread offense that Clemson would install under Morris. Dabo told Watson that they would build the entire program around him.

But Watson wasn't ready to commit. In the fall of 2011, during his sophomore season, he visited several schools, including Alabama, Florida, Georgia, and Tennessee. He also traveled to Clemson six more times to watch its games and verify that he would in fact flourish in Morris's offense. On February 1, 2012, Watson committed to the Tigers via a post on Facebook.

Dabo and Watson grew close. The quarterback shared his background with Dabo: Watson grew up one of four children to a single mom in government housing. As a kid, he played football in a grassy area of the Harrison Square Apartments, but he saw drugs, gangs, and fighting nearly every day. Then one morning, Habitat for Humanity contacted his mom, Deann, and told her that they would help her move out of unit A4 at Harrison Square and they would assist her in building her own house. She immediately said yes and agreed that she and her family would work three hundred hours on the house.

Little Deshaun hammered nails, helped paint walls, and watched his mom work until the point of exhaustion. Seeing her ethic profoundly affected Deshaun: It changed his attitude toward life. He decided then that he would pour his heart and soul into school and sports, giving full effort every day in everything he did. The Watsons were handed the keys to the house two days before Thanksgiving in 2006. Upon entering the front door, they found the house complete with furniture, kitchen supplies, beds, even artwork on the walls. Warrick

Dunn, then a running back for the Atlanta Falcons, had paid for everything. Deann was overcome with emotion.

Now living in a middle-class neighborhood, Deshaun no longer had to worry about drug deals or gun-wielding gang members hanging out just feet from his front door. His life would never be the same. Now he could concentrate on what was really important. When Dabo heard Deshaun tell his story, he became more convinced than ever that Deshaun would be a program-changing player for the Tigers. He believed he had the character and the comportment of a winner. Dabo didn't say it, but Deshaun had a healthy dose of Dabo in him.

Even after Deshaun pledged to attend Clemson, the top schools such as Florida State, Auburn, Ohio State, and Alabama kept coming after Watson, wooing him. He was named the Georgia State player of the year his final three seasons of high school. Though Gainesville was only a forty-five-minute drive from the Georgia campus, the Bulldogs were late to offer Watson a scholarship. Then again, every school was late compared to the Tigers.

IN MAY 2015, BIG Erv moved to Clemson and lived in Dabo's basement. Dabo and Kathleen convinced him to undergo eight weeks of radiation and chemotherapy for lung cancer in Greenville and not Birmingham. Never one to waste an opportunity, Dabo used this time to really get to know his dad, to tighten their bond.

They talked long into many nights, rehashing some of the good times they had: the trip to New Orleans the family took to watch their beloved Crimson Tide, the afternoons spent in the living room transfixed by *The Bear Bryant Show*. Dabo never stopped believing in his father, even when Big Erv was in the vise grip of his alcoholism. There were times when Kathleen didn't want to be around Dabo's father, but Dabo steadfastly refused to give up hope. He'd say, "Dad, you need to do this. You need to accept Christ in your life."

Ervil was happy to be living with his son in Clemson, surrounded by family. His son Tracy, who had been a police officer in Alabama, moved to Clemson to be with Dabo. Now that their dad was in town, the family would go to dinner together and make up for lost time—lost years. Dabo or his brother would take their dad to the hospital and then spend up to eight hours with him as he received his chemotherapy treatments. Big Erv would talk to his boys about everything— like Dabo, he was a gifted storyteller and could yammer on with the best of them. Dabo took his dad for rides in his truck, a time for more talking. They attended baseball and flag football games together and sat side by side in Dabo's truck that he parked near the field—the bleachers were too hot for Big Erv—as they watched Dabo's boys. They plopped down in front of the television together in their boxers and talked family and football. They seemingly did everything they could to recapture the relationship they had early in Dabo's youth— a youth cut short by Big Erv's battle with the bottle.

When Big Erv moved back to Birmingham once the treatments were completed, Dabo would often be in his truck on Sundays and call his dad. "What are you doing?" he'd ask.

"Oh, I ain't doing nothing," Ervil would say. "What are you doing?"

"Aw, just riding home, checkin' on you," Dabo would say.

After spending time with Dabo and his son's family, Big Erv told Dabo, *The good Lord can take me right now. I'm at peace with everything.*

Three weeks after leaving his son's basement, as he waited for test results to see if the cancer had been eradicated or if it had returned, Ervil went back to work at M&M Hardware, where he repaired washers and dryers. An eight-by-eleven picture of Dabo standing by Howard's Rock at Memorial Stadium hung behind the cash register, a gift that Dabo had given him with the inscription that read, "Thanks for showing me the way. I am so proud of you! I love you! Dabo."

Ervil was so happy and grateful for the time he had been able to spend with Dabo and Tracy and the rest of the family in Clemson. He told his friends that he felt as healthy as ever. Then, on August 8, 2015, as he was sitting in his chair behind his desk at the hardware store—not far from that picture of his boy—he stopped breathing. He died a contented man at age seventy.

Dabo loved his dad dearly and believed he was a great man who had fought hard to overcome his demons. He detests it when reporters portray his father as a bad person when telling his story. Dabo acknowledges the fact that Big Erv's behavior had been destructive when Dabo was young, but Dabo believed his father was a redeemed man who had always tried his best, even when he was coming up short.

Dabo was at his house on Lake Keowee—a man-made reservoir in South Carolina with three hundred miles of shoreline—with his family when the news was delivered over the phone. That night he drove Big Erv's truck over to his mom's house—she also lived in Clemson—to be with her and cry with her and begin the process of mourning. Before he left for Alabama to say his final good-bye to his dad, Dabo met with his team. The players could see that their coach was hurting—"We all just wanted to go up and hug him," said one player—and then Dabo flew to Birmingham. At the funeral in Pelham, Dabo delivered a long, heartfelt eulogy. His dad was put into the ground at Elmwood Cemetery, not too far from Bear Bryant.

The next day, Dabo returned to Clemson and told staffers that his father, who had been a hard-working man for the majority of his life, would want his son to get back at it and immediately restart the grind. Life was too short for extended mourning. "All right, that's enough," Dabo said his father would demand. "Get yourself back to work. We have some football games to win."

In his office, Dabo had a picture of Big Erv that he looked at every day. It showed his dad at a Clemson game at Death Valley, his arms raised in jubilation, celebrating the team coached by his boy—a portrait of a proud father.

ON OCTOBER 3, 2015—about two months after his dad's death—Clemson faced Notre Dame in what would become known as the BYOG (Bring Your Own Guts) game. The

Fighting Irish hadn't visited Clemson since 1977 when Dan Devine was the coach and Joe Montana was the quarterback, and the demand for tickets was unlike any other home game of the Swinney era. "I couldn't get Jesus tickets," he joked to reporters. "I've got people calling me I hadn't talked to in 20 years. 'Hey man, got some tickets? I really want to come this weekend. Just need...five.'"

A few days before kickoff against the Irish, Dabo saw a piece of grass growing in a crack in the concrete steps at Memorial Stadium. He took a mental snapshot of that grass blade, and, as Dabo often does, he turned it into a metaphor and built a team talk around one of his favorite aphorisms: *Bloom where you're planted. Don't let circumstances seal your fate. Rise to the challenge and overcome the odds.* These words were similar to those he had spoken to C.J. Spiller years earlier when he convinced his star running back to stay at Clemson instead of transferring to Florida—an act that surely contributed to Dabo being the head coach at Clemson now.

Clemson was 3-0 and ranked No. 12 in the polls; Notre Dame was ranked sixth. College GameDay was in town and the game would be on national television. This was a touchstone moment for Dabo and the Tigers. They had won bowl games and ACC titles and beaten powerhouse programs such as Ohio State, LSU, and Oklahoma—the term *Clemsoning* was about to be put out to pasture for good—and this was Dabo's chance to take a giant leap forward and put his program in the conversation for being one of the nation's most consistent and best. The players felt this way because of Notre Dame's rich tradition. "That game was, 'Oh, we're here. We can make this run,'" recalled offensive lineman Eric Mac Lain, a senior that season.

And then…the rain came, a driving storm that was triggered by Hurricane Joaquin. It was an Old Testament style of drenching, an all-day soaker so intense it seemed created by a Hollywood special effects team. When Notre Dame coach Brian Kelly walked out onto the field before the game, he gazed up into the stands and saw the seats filled with fans in ponchos and slickers. His eyes grew wide: He couldn't believe that the Clemson faithful showed up in such inclement weather.

Behind the play of Deshaun Watson and several other big-time recruits that Dabo had lured to Clemson, including defensive tackle Christian Wilkins (who recorded his first sack as a Tiger in the game and would go on to be a first-round NFL draft pick) and linebacker Shaq Lawson (also a future first-round NFL draft pick), Clemson jumped to a 21–3 lead early in the third quarter. And the Tigers held on to win 24–22.

As soon as the clock expired, fans swarmed Dabo as ESPN sideline reporter Heather Cox interviewed him. Dabo shouted above the din. "It ain't always perfect, but what I told them tonight was, 'Listen, we give you scholarships. We give you stipends, meals, a place to live. We give you nice uniforms.'" Dabo's voice rose a few octaves. "'I can't give you guts. I can't give you heart. Tonight, hey, it was BYOG—Bring Your Own Guts!' And they brought some guts and some heart and they never quit."

In the locker room, Dabo danced like no one was watching, performing in front of his team the Nae Nae—hips gyrating, eyes bulging, arms flying—reinforcing his image to his players as the dorky dad they didn't want to disappoint. Both his speech and dance went viral on social media, enhancing his growing reputation as a coach who loved to have fun. How important was this victory? In their previous three games against teams ranked in the AP Top 25, Clemson was winless and had been outscored 96–44.

Tigertown Graphics sold nearly fifteen thousand T-shirts emblazoned with the letters BYOG. The letters were soon also imprinted on hats, shirts, sweaters, and other items. It wasn't the first time that Dabo had dug up an acronym.

By this point he had PAW (Passionate About Winning), A.L.L.I.N (Attitude, Leadership, Legacy, Improvement, New Beginnings) and BYOE (Bring Your Own Energy). These acronyms can come off as over-the-top and a little corny, but not to his players. To them, they represented what Dabo and Clemson football were all about.

SUNDAY NIGHTS WERE THE most difficult for Dabo during the 2015 season. Father and son had a ritual to talk on Sunday evenings after games, with Big Erv usually telling Dabo, "Boy, I'm so proud of you," and then he'd discuss the game. Dabo always looked forward to these conversations—they connected him to his dad—and now he missed them oh so much. Even a forty-six-year-old man, one with more money than he ever dreamed he'd have, seeks the approval of his father.

Dabo kept four voice mail messages from his father on his cell phone. He listened to them often during the season. They brought him comfort as Clemson raced to a 13-0 record, an ACC championship, and a spot in the College Football Playoffs, where the Tigers would face Oklahoma in the semifinals. Clemson entered the playoffs ranked No. 1 and was the nation's only undefeated team. Dabo was the Associated Press Coach of the Year, Walter Camp Coach of the Year, and Home Depot Coach of the Year, and he won the Paul "Bear" Bryant award for being the nation's most outstanding coach—a collection of hardware that no other coach in Clemson history accumulated in a single season.

And yet there still was a kind of hollowness in Dabo's heart because he couldn't enjoy the success with his dad. "It's been a spiritual season for me," Dabo told reporters before facing Oklahoma in the Orange Bowl on New Year's Eve. "I can sense his happiness and his peace and his smiles. I can just see him tailgating in heaven right now with his Clemson buddies up there happy for his son and rooting hard and talking trash, if they allow that in heaven. It's been a peaceful and comforting year for me in that regard."

THE BIGGEST SURPRISE OF the 2015 season had been the play of the Clemson defense. When Brent Venables was hired in 2012, he installed a blitzing, 4-3 scheme that featured multiple looks. It took him a few years to recruit the players he needed to turn the defense into an elite group—too often in 2012 and 2013 Clemson had to outscore opponents—but by 2014 the Tigers had the top-ranked defensive unit in the nation, one filled with five- and four-star recruits. The defense was a reflection of their coach, a man so intense that he chews five different flavors of gum on the sideline during games, a coach who against South Carolina during the 2014 season had to be held back by another assistant from running onto the field and jumping on the ball after a strip-sack that caused a fumble a few feet from the Clemson sideline.

The 2015 version of the Tiger D was nearly as dominate, finishing sixth in the nation in yards per game (301.6). After defeating Notre Dame, Clemson went on a roll, defeating the likes of Miami (58–0), Florida State (23–13), and North Carolina (45–37) in the ACC title game to cap the school's first undefeated regular season since Clemson won the national title in 1981. They were ranked No. 1 entering the College Football Playoffs, where the Tigers faced Oklahoma in the national semifinals.

At one practice during the team's preparation for the Sooners, Venables was playing the role of Sooner quarterback Baker Mayfield when 270-pound defensive end Shaq Lawson accidently steamrolled Venables, who quickly popped up off the ground with an I-love-this smile on his face. As they had all season, the players would feed off their coach's wild-eyed intensity in the playoffs.

Watson powered the offense. He became the first Clemson player to be a Heisman finalist. He finished third behind winner Derrick Henry, an Alabama running back, and runner-up Christian McCaffrey, a running back from Stanford. But

Watson became the first player in the history of college football to throw for over 4,000 yards and rush for over 1,000 yards—and he did it only as a sophomore. Watson was everything Dabo thought he would be when he recruited him.

In the national semifinal, with Watson and the Clemson offense struggling early in the game, Dabo displayed his inner gambler. Trailing Oklahoma 7–3 in the second quarter, Clemson faced a fourth and four from Sooners' 44-yard line. Dabo called a fake punt named UConn. The play required junior punter Andy Teasdall to throw a pass, even though Dabo hadn't exactly been pleased with Teasdall the last time Clemson had been on the football field in the ACC championship against North Carolina. During that game, Teasdall had ad-libbed a fake punt and failed to make a first down. Dabo ripped Teasdall at halftime to the sideline reporter for overruling him and berated him again in the media after the game.

But Dabo never said he didn't believe in his punter—he knew his punter well enough to know he could handle criticism—and afterward he privately told Teasdall that he cared for him and was going to need him to make plays moving forward. Teasdall's shot at redemption arrived against Oklahoma when Dabo called "UConn." Lining up in regular punt formation, Teasdall received the snap. But instead of kicking the ball, the punter threw a pass to 315-pound freshman defensive tackle Christian Wilkins (who went to high school in Connecticut, the basis for the name of the play) and he ran 31 yards down the sideline.

The tone and tenor of the game was never the same—the play shell-shocked the Sooners. Clemson went on to win 37–17. After the game, Dabo told reporters, "We ain't no underdogs." They would face a school in the national title game that was located about three hundred miles west of Clemson on Interstate 20, a school that Dabo knew well, one that had won three of the previous five national championships: Alabama.

FIVE DAYS AFTER DISMANTLING Oklahoma, Dabo met with the media in Glendale, Arizona, site of the championship matchup. He went on and on about how much he admired Bear Bryant and how much he loved the Crimson Tide as a boy growing up in Alabama. "You leave the hospital, they stamp your birth certificate Alabama or Auburn," Dabo said. "That's just how it is."

Dabo relished his role as an outsider. He described his team as "the rednecks who moved into a nice neighborhood, and everyone's wondering who the hell they are." Dabo's longtime mentor Woody McCorvey said, "This is a matchup [Dabo has] always wanted."

ON THE MORNING OF the game, Alabama's Nick Saban met with kicker Adam Griffith in a conference room at the team hotel. In his dozens of hours of film study during the week, Saban had noticed that when Clemson expected a kickoff to be directed deep and to one corner of the field, the entire Tiger return unit shifted to that side of the field. Saban explained to Griffith that if he saw Clemson line up like that early in the game, it could create the opportunity for an onside kick late.

On the first four Alabama kickoffs, the Tigers lined up the way Saban wanted—all shifted to the right side of the field, leaving about 12 yards of open space on the opposite side. But each time Saban opted against trying the onside kick. Like a card player holding royal flush, Saban didn't want to show his hand until he absolutely had to. Then the moment of the game—and the season—arrived.

Tied at 24 in the fourth quarter and his defense struggling to contain Clemson quarterback Deshaun Watson, Saban believed the time was right. Normally risk-averse, Saban made a gutsy call—it was time to try the pop onside kick. The target of the play, cornerback Marlon Humphrey, had dropped the ball in the team's walk-through practice before the game, but this didn't deter Saban. Neither did the fact that surprise onside kicks in college football, according to various analytics, are successful only about 40 percent of the time.

Griffith approached the tee slower than normal, but that didn't alert any of the Clemson players. He pooched the ball toward the right sideline in a perfect arc. With no Tiger defender within 3 yards of him, Humphrey caught the ball in the stride at the 50-yard line. The successful trick prompted a rare, I-got-you grin from Saban on the sideline as Dabo screamed at the referees, even though nothing about the play was illegal. It was as if Dabo had realized, at this moment, that he had been hoodwinked and out-coached by Saban. Two plays later, Tide quarterback Jake Coker connected with tight end O.J. Howard down the left sideline for a 51-yard touch-down. Alabama ended the night with sixteen possessions; the Tigers had fifteen. The onside kick was the key play in Alabama's 45–40 win.

Facing the greatest college football dynasty of the twenty-first century, Clemson had scored 40 points. The Tigers gained 550 yards of offense. Dabo and the Tigers, who hadn't lost since November 2014, were one game-changing play call from possibly taking down Alabama, who had just won its fourth national title in seven years. Clemson showed it belonged on the field. "Where is this thing next year? Is it in Tampa?" Dabo asked that night. "We'll see if we can reload and go do it again."

After the postgame press conference, Dabo went back into the locker room and hugged a few former players who were lingering inside. "I'm sorry we didn't get it done," he said. "We'll be back."

Dabo returned to his hotel room around 2:00 a.m. He was too juiced to sleep, even though the team had an early morning flight across the country. He got into bed and turned on the television. A replay of the game was just starting.

Dabo watched every painful minute. He questioned a few of the calls he made. He analyzed every mistake that could have changed the final score. He fumed at the onside kick call by Saban. But his overwhelming feeling was that of gratitude—gratitude that he was able to be in such an important game, gratitude that his players gave such great effort, gratitude that from 2011 to 2015 he had won fifty-six games and had a winning percentage (.824) that was second only to Saban's (.899). He knew that the players believed in him and in his vision. He believed with all his heart that the coming dawn would be bright and brilliant for Clemson football.

When the replay of the game was over, Dabo packed his belongings into his travel bag and headed to the lobby. In the shadow of such a crushing defeat, he was a contented man. Deep down, deep in that place that is the wellspring of all his positive energy, he knew the best was yet to come.

CHAPTER 8

RELIGION, RECRUITING, AND THE RIGHT-HAND MAN

In 2007, Dabo and his family began attending NewSpring Church in Anderson, South Carolina, a Southern Baptist megachurch founded in 2000, located fifteen miles from the Clemson campus. The pastor at NewSpring at the time was Perry Noble. It didn't take long for Dabo, an evangelical Christian, and Noble to develop a close relationship. Before and after games, Noble would send Dabo text messages that featured words and wonder from the Good Book. Noble became so intertwined with Tiger football that—as Dabo and other coaches sometimes watched—he baptized several Clemson players, including star wide receiver Sammy Watkins and defensive end Malliciah Goodman.

They say that football is religion in the South, but that's just an aphorism that underscores the passion of college football fans. At Dabo's Clemson, though, religion plays a prominent role in the program. Before he accepted the position of wide receivers coach from Tommy Bowden in 2002, Dabo and Bowden prayed together about the decision, asking for His wisdom to guide them toward the light of the correct path. Dabo hadn't always been a devout Christian—as a kid, his mom basically had to force him to go to church—but then in high school he attended a Fellowship of Christian Athletes meeting at which the keynote speaker was Joey Jones, a former Alabama wide receiver who was one of his idols.

"I thought he was going to talk about touchdowns and all the money he made playing for the Falcons and for the USFL [Birmingham] Stallions," Dabo said. "All he talked about was his faith in Christ and his relationship there. If you're not saved and want to be saved here's what you have to do. I realized I wasn't saved. Joe Jones led me to the Lord that night."

Since that meeting, Dabo hasn't avoided discussing his faith with players, fans, and administrators. When Dabo arrived at Clemson, head coach Tommy Bowden encouraged his assistants to act as spiritual advisors to their players— to metaphorically hold their hand and, if they asked, show them the way to the Lord. Dabo quickly connected to the players. He shared stories from his turbulent past, discussed how the Lord guided him through the darkness, encouraged him and kept him pushing forward, even when times were the hardest. He told his players that his relationship with the Lord was the reason he was able to overcome his challenges and failures. One receiver observed that, at certain times, Dabo could have been mistaken for a Baptist preacher, the way the words about his passion for Christ flowed from his mouth as naturally as water from a spring. Dabo always had the gift of gab, but nothing got his silver tongue wagging like it did when he talked about his Lord and Savior and how He had guided him through the storms of his life and into a wondrous sunlight.

Dabo had players over to his house, where he would ask them about their families, their studies, their hopes and their fears. Often these discussions would veer into the topic of God, and Dabo would share how he was saved and how he had turned his will and his life over to his Higher Power. He emphasized that the only reason he was where he was now in life was because of the Lord, how He had led him and his family to Clemson. He spoke about the spiritual balance and the peace that was within him.

As an assistant coach, Dabo invited his receivers to go to church with him, sometimes giving them a ride to NewSpring Baptist. If Dabo saw a player going down a wrong path, he'd call that player into his office and deliver a one-on-one sermon, trying to save a soul as much as set the player straight. He'd tell a player, "Have you ever thought about giving your life to Christ? Everything else will fall into place. You get your health right, you get your spirituality right, everything else falls into place." He told his straying players about a routine they should embrace: get up early, read the Bible, pray, and attend church as much as possible.

Once Dabo became head coach, he began treating his entire roster the way he had his wide receivers. Now instead of merely using his Christianity and his own personal story to cultivate relationships with his wide receiver group, he openly spoke to the entire team about his faith and how it had sustained him. Dabo prayed frequently during the day, sometimes asking other players to join him.

Dabo also hired devoutly religious coaches, including Jeff Scott and Brent Venables. He hired Jeff Davis—a Hall of Fame linebacker on the '81 Clemson title team and a pastor at a local church—as director of player relations. He eventually hired former Clemson player James Trapp to be the team chaplain. Dabo then did something rare: He made Trapp a bona fide Clemson employee and paid him a salary, which meant he could talk to recruits without breaking any NCAA rules—an act that the vast majority of public universities would never allow. But it was important for Dabo to surround himself with believers. Coaches in all sports and in all regions of the country talk about religion; Dabo lives it, breathes it, and isn't afraid to discuss it even during team meetings.

But Dabo is quick to dispel the notion that religion plays a role in how Clemson judges a potential recruit. "My job is to win football games," Dabo said during a press conference before the 2015 Orange Bowl. "We're always going to recruit and play the best football players....We don't play the best Christians. I've said that many times. If we were playing the best Christians, I wouldn't be sitting here, I can guarantee you that. I just know how I'm called to live my life. I try to be consistent with that. Be who you are, whatever you are. I've coached a bunch of atheists I'm sure. Along the way, a ton."

Dabo expanded on this subject in June 2020 during a Fellowship of Christian Athletes conference call. "I always tell everybody, my job is not to save 'em," he said. "My job is to win football games. I've come under fire many times from different organizations and things like that because of my faith. They want me to just shut that off and not be a Christian. But God says in Colossians 3:23, 'Whatever you do, you do it with all your heart as if you're working for the Lord.'"

He continued during that call, streamed live on YouTube. "If I get a young man that comes to Clemson, and he's strong in his faith, and he leaves Clemson and I didn't help him grow stronger, shame on me. If I get a young man that comes to Clemson, and he doesn't know anything, or he's searching, and I don't cultivate that...Shame on me...

"I hope [my players] see Christ in me as I do my job. I hope that they see the light of Jesus through me as I do my job that God's called me to do...We're called to love people. We're called to serve people. And our whole philosophy of our program is to serve the heart and not their talent."

ONE STORY: AFTER THE game where Clemson beat North Carolina 59–38 on October 29, 2011—a win that lifted Clemson's record to 8-0—Dabo raised his hand in the locker room. The players fell quiet as Dabo told his young men about the 1981 Clemson team that had won the national championship and how they also started the season 8-0. "You are on the verge of greatness," he said, "but you've got to kick the door down."

He then asked the players and coaches to hold hands in

the locker room. "We thank of the good Lord for the privilege of being on this team," he said. "Help us be a team and love each other." He prayed that everyone would make sound decisions on this Saturday night and that everyone would be safe. "I pray that the people will know that we have Christ among us." He sounded like a preacher, and nearly everyone in his congregation had their heads bowed as he spoke.

The last player to leave the locker room was Dwayne Allen, a senior tight end who was savoring this moment. Allen had sparred with the coaching staff during his time at Clemson, once telling a coach to "f--- off" and another time refusing to step foot on the practice field. After those incidents and knowing that Allen came from a poor home in Fayetteville, North Carolina, Dabo opened up to Allen, telling him how the Lord had uplifted and guided him. The talk was a turning point for Allen, who afterward became one of the hardest working, most admired players on the team.

"What I experienced under Coach Swinney was a total transformation," Allen said. Allen wasn't religious, but the praying never bothered him. Instead, he listened to the messages that Dabo was delivering, not the fact that they were given in the context of religion. Allen said that he and Dabo shared a "love" for each other and that without Dabo and his constant encouragement, he didn't know where he'd be.

ANOTHER STORY: THE FOLLOWING year, in August 2012, Clemson had just finished a preseason practice on a hot summer day when a few assistant coaches dragged a few ice tubs onto the field. Dabo blew his whistle and asked the players to gather around him. He said that DeAndre Hopkins, the team's top receiver and a future first-round draft pick, would be getting baptized in a few minutes right here on the practice field. He told his players they could stick around for the ceremony if they wished or they could head to the locker room.

Nearly everyone stayed. The players and assistants moved around one of the ice tubs, which was brimming with water. Still in his uniform and pads, Hopkins stepped into the tub. "Jesus is the most important thing in my life," Hopkins said, "and I want you guys to know that I'm living for him." A pastor from a nearby Baptist Church then baptized him. The players and coaches applauded and yelled like they themselves were experiencing some sort of rapture. A coach got so caught up in the moment that he tweeted a photo of Hopkins's baptism, a picture that featured coaches clapping and cheering on Hopkins.

By April 2014, the Freedom From Religion Foundation (FFRF)—a nonprofit organization that promotes the separation of church and state—had received a few complaints about Hopkins's baptism. A lawyer for FFRF then sent Clemson a letter stating the First Amendment prohibited a public institution such as Clemson from promoting Christianity. The organization believed that the team's Bible studies, coach-led team prayers, baptisms, and organized church trips violated the First Amendment.

Clemson said it would investigate the complaint, but no major changes to how Dabo ran his football program or how Clemson itself embraced Christianity were ever made. "You're not drafted to Clemson," said Dan Radakovich, the school's athletic director in 2015. "You have choices and you choose to come and go to this academic institution and you choose to play for these coaches." After the FFRF report became public, Dabo spoke at a team meeting. He told his players that if any of them felt uncomfortable about anything, they should "please come talk to me about it so I can see your side of it." Not one player went to talk to the coach, but a question remained: Would a player be brave enough to share his concerns with his head coach who ultimately controlled his playing time and, thus, his football future?

And yet Dabo has never had a single player tell him—or anyone on his staff—that his wear-it-on-my-sleeve Christianity has made him feel uncomfortable, not even players with different beliefs. Aaron Kelly played wide receiver for Dabo when he was his position coach and then when Dabo was head coach. A Jehovah's Witness, Kelly didn't attend team Bible studies or attend church with other players or coaches, but he said he never felt alienated. "You just knew that that's something that was important to him," Kelly said. "It wasn't something he hid or shied away from. You knew it up front, but it was nothing that he ever forced on us and made us feel like we had to do that."

The first time Kelly told his coach that he wouldn't be able to participate in a religious activity with the team, he was filled with anxiety, unsure of how Dabo would react. But all he felt from his coach was one thing: love. "We all have our beliefs,"

Dabo told him, "and I want you to feel comfortable." When asked if he thought his coach ever held his beliefs against him, Kelly was quick to point out that he was a four-year starter for Dabo.

DeAndre Hopkins was a three-year starter for Dabo before being the twenty-seventh overall pick in the 2013 NFL draft by the Houston Texans. A year after Hopkins got baptized, the team chaplain, James Trapp, taught voluntary workshops inside the main football building about what it meant to get baptized and giving yourself to the Lord. Hopkins was the team's top player and—whether inspired by him or the words of the team chaplain or by Dabo—many decided to follow Hopkins's religious lead. From 2013 to 2015, one former player estimated that ten to fifteen of his teammates were baptized in a pond on campus.

At Clemson, the good word is indeed powerful.

MAKE NO MISTAKE: DABO and his staff use religion in recruiting. When Dabo interacts with a recruit, he sometimes will emphasize spiritual development as much as he does physical, academic, and social growth. Dabo doesn't question the faith of the players he recruits, but he sometimes conveys his own belief system by telling tidbits from his past, which in effect is a faith-based pitch to recruits.

In 2019, D.J. Uiagalelei, the top quarterback recruit in the class of 2020, flew from his hometown of Bellflower, California, to visit Clemson, where he toured the campus and chatted with coaches and players. Nearly everyone Uiagalelei interacted with openly discussed their relationship with their Lord and Savior and how Dabo had built a team of believers and a culture of faith. Uiagalelei—himself a believer in Christ—called his mom and said, "You can feel the presence of God here. He's here, Mom. He's here." Another talented quarterback, Deshaun Watson, said that Dabo's beliefs were one reason why he chose to play at Clemson. "It was part of it, of course," Watson said, "[to] know that my coach is a Man of God." Quarterback Trevor Lawrence was baptized in a small ceremony at NewSpring at the beginning of his first year at Clemson.

During Uiagalelei's official recruiting visit to Clemson, Dabo met with D.J.'s mom, Tausha. They talked about their common religious views, and then he made a promise to her. "We're going to win some games and lose some games," Dabo told her. "But I guarantee you that every single player that comes through this program will hear about the Gospel of Christ."

Uiagalelei signed with Clemson. The primary reason? Dabo's commitment to Christ.

A MAN BLESSED WITH a long memory, Dabo once heard someone say that a dead battery can't charge another dead battery, because it doesn't have any juice. This metaphor stuck with him. Now he intentionally surrounds himself with people who charge his spirit and his attitude.

One of those is Thad Turnipseed, who played linebacker at Alabama and was Dabo's teammate from 1990 to 1992. The two became especially close when they shared a small, ten-foot-by-ten-foot office in the Crimson Tide football facility in 1993 and 1994 when Dabo was a graduate assistant and Turnipseed—who had to quit playing due to serious knee injuries—was a student assistant. After graduating from Alabama in 1995 with a degree in political science and a double minor in geology and general business, Turnipseed went into construction, owning his own business. He returned to work at Alabama in 2002 as the director of intercollegiate capital projects—he oversaw the expansion of Bryant–Denny Stadium—and in 2007 he started to work closely with Nick Saban, becoming, in essence, his right-hand man. Saban began calling Turnipseed "director of external football affairs," and his responsibilities ranged from overseeing more than $200 million in capital projects to event planning, fundraising, and recruiting.

Turnipseed didn't have a role in anything that related to the actual playing of football, but he had a hand in virtually everything else. Staffers joked that his title should have been "Keep Nick Happy" because he did so many things for Saban, including building an expansive room in Saban's house that became known as the Recruiting Room, a place where Saban takes recruits when they visit Tuscaloosa.

Turnipseed was with Saban on the morning of April 28, 2011, only hours after a vicious tornado had ripped through Tuscaloosa, killing more than fifty, including six students. The two drove a pickup truck into the hardest hit areas. Turnipseed watched as Saban handed out water and hugs to the victims and first responders who frantically dug through the rubble searching for survivors. This day had a profound impact on Saban—he embraced more people in a twelve-hour period than he had during the entirety of his life, and it wound up deepening his roots in Alabama, solidifying his role as a leader in the community. He was no longer merely a coach; he was a figure that people looked to for comfort and support. This day changed everything for Saban, and Turnipseed witnessed it all from behind the wheel of the pickup truck.

For several years, in fact, Turnipseed had a front-row seat to all that Saban did, enabling him to closely watch and understand how Saban had built his empire in T-Town. He saw what ingredients Saban had thrown into his secret sauce and how Saban had cooked it. In 2013, Dabo called his old teammate and officemate and offered Turnipseed a job. Turnipseed's first question: What do you want me to do?

"Thad, I don't care what you do," Dabo replied. "I don't care if you don't want to do anything for a year. Just come. Learn. Be around. When you see something that can make us better, make us better and go to the next thing."

On his way home from the interview, Turnipseed called his wife and detailed how the day had gone. "We're going to Clemson, aren't we?" she asked.

"All I can tell you, honey, is that it's real," Turnipseed replied.

Early in his tenure at Clemson, Turnipseed was surprised to see Dabo hugging players, talking to them about their families, and cutting up with them like he was a player himself. This was a far cry from Saban's Alabama, where the culture was geared toward two things and two things only: winning and developing players for the NFL. There was a more businesslike approach in Tuscaloosa than the family-oriented, let's-have-fun culture at Dabo's Clemson. "Just a totally different atmosphere at Clemson than it was at Alabama," said Turnipseed, who at the time had four young children. "I'm not saying better. I'm saying different. That atmosphere at Clemson, for a guy with young kids, a young family, was the right fit for me at the time."

The building of a grand, sweeping, new-age football facility was just in the planning stages when Turnipseed arrived at Clemson that June. So Turnipseed—a man with a soaring imagination who would play a key role in designing that facility—focused on recruiting and was eventually given the title of director of recruiting and external affairs. Turnipseed's fingerprints quickly were all over Clemson's recruiting efforts. The Tigers' recruiting war room was modeled after Alabama's. Recruits were tracked on dry-erase boards for three years, six at each position. The Tiger staff conducted checks on the character of each player they were targeting. If a red flag was raised, that recruit was erased from the board—even if he was a five star. Staffers monitored the social media behavior of potential recruits and ranked them by character.

"Sometimes I've been around coordinators that don't like to recruit," Dabo said. "Everybody's got good Xs and Os, and everybody's got good coaches. It's getting the great players. That's your lifeline. Our entire staff is structured that way."

But the ultimate closer on the staff is Dabo. When he speaks to a recruit and his family, he already has done his homework on the prospect and understands what makes him tick.

He'll connect with the recruit by telling a tale from his past—something that is relatable to the prospect's own experience—and then he'll lay out a clear vision for the recruit's future, for how he'll develop him as a player and a person over the next few years at Clemson. Always maintaining eye contact, always smiling, always speaking in a caring voice, and always quick to spin a fascinating yarn, Dabo excels at selling dreams—the skill he honed when he was a real estate leasing agent.

Turnipseed was in awe of Dabo's recruiting ability. After watching Saban for so many years, Turnipseed believed there were three keys to being a successful head coach: intelligence, the ability to command respect from players and coaches, and to be feared. At first Turnipseed worried that Dabo was too nice, that his players weren't appropriately afraid of him the way players were of Saban, who ruled with an iron fist; if you didn't do things the way he wanted, he either showed you the door or made your life miserable. But then Turnipseed, after seeing Dabo with his players in different settings, realized that Dabo motivated his players in way that was far different from his former boss. Turnipseed said, "People are just afraid to disappoint Dabo."

Therein lies yet another secret of Dabo: Unlike many coaches who inspired players by creating fear, Dabo motivated his players by a concept he would frequently talk about in the coming years, a one-word description that distilled the essence of all that he was trying to cultivate and instill—for better or worse—at Clemson:

Love.

CHAPTER 9

DABO'S FIRST TITLE

After returning to Clemson following the national championship game loss to Alabama, Dabo had a banner hung in the indoor practice facility that read "National Finalist." This was not intended to celebrate the Tigers' trip to the Arizona desert and its oh-so-close loss to the Crimson Tide. No, the unfurling of these two words—*National Finalist*—was designed to remind his players that they still had work to do if they wanted to summit the college football mountaintop. "Coach did a great job of putting that in our face," said linebacker Ben Boulware.

Midway through the spring of 2016, Dabo liked the collective mindset and approach of his team. Like every coach, Dabo punished his players who broke team rules, such as being late for class, falling behind in their academic responsibilities, or wearing the wrong workout attire in the weight room. The penalty for these minor indiscretions was what

Dabo called his "accountability runs," also widely known as extra sprints. But for the first three dates of the runs that spring, not a single player had to participate in those grueling tests of endurance, because none had violated a team rule. That had never happened since Dabo became head coach, and it led him to believe that his players were as focused as ever on football—a sign of their desperate desire to be one game better than they had been in 2015.

Every coach uses motivational techniques, and Dabo is no different. Former UCLA basketball coach John Wooden, who won ten championships over a twelve-year period, is regarded as one of the best motivators of all time in any sport. Of the many things he insisted on, one of the most important was that his players be unselfish. "I believe that every basketball team is a unit, and I didn't separate my players as to starters and subs," said Wooden after he retired in 1975 (and passed away in 2010). "I tried to make it clear that every man plays a role, including the coach, assistants, the trainer, and the managers."

Dabo knew he had the potential to have a special group of players for the upcoming 2016 season. The prospective roster was littered with former four- and five-star players. Twelve starters returned from the team that was the national runner-up in 2015, including quarterback Deshaun Watson. Plus, wide receiver Mike Williams, a future first-round draft pick who suffered a neck injury in the first game of the 2015 season and missed the rest of the year, was healthy and would be back. And Dabo had continuity on his coaching staff that was the envy of head coaches around the nation; none of his top assistants had left his side in the previous two years. This 2016 team, Dabo knew, was built to win it all.

Each season Dabo chooses a single word that he hopes will bond the team together and serve as the program's motto for the upcoming season. Trying to get his players to continually operate as a "unit"—Wooden's word—and to always think about how the greater good of the team outweighed the singular happiness of any individual, Dabo chose the word *love*. He couldn't explain precisely why he picked that word, other than to say, "That's just something that was put on my spirit. When you love something, you just want to give that little extra."

At the most critical moment of the 2016 season, at the defining moment of his coaching career, Dabo would draw on the immeasurable power of this word—*love*—over and over and over again.

ON OCTOBER 1, 2016, the colorful set of ESPN's College GameDay arose in Death Valley in preparation for the broadcast of No. 5 ranked Clemson's widely anticipated matchup against No. 3 Louisville, a team that featured Lamar Jackson, the eventual Heisman Trophy winner. The producers at GameDay invited Dabo to join the crew on the stage at Bowman Field on Clemson's campus. A state trooper picked Dabo up from the team hotel in Anderson, South Carolina, and drove him to the ESPN set. After his segment was over, Dabo returned to the patrol car and the trooper began driving back to Anderson.

With blue and red lights flashing, the trooper motored along Perimeter Road, the stadium sitting in the near distance. Looking out the window, Dabo spotted fans already tailgating at about 10:00 a.m., even though the game wasn't scheduled to begin for nearly ten hours—8:22 p.m. They were drinking beer, cooking hot dogs and hamburgers on grills, tossing around footballs, and lounging in fold-out orange camping chairs.

"Man, pull over right here," Dabo told the state trooper.

Dabo approached a group that was sitting outside a large orange van. "Hey, boys, we ready to go?" Dabo said. "Y'all drinking beer already? It's gone be rockin' in the Valley tonight."

At first, the fans fell into stunned silence at the sight of their coach. They thought they had done something wrong and were in trouble, but Dabo assured them that he was there only to greet them and thank them for their support. Dabo then kept walking, visiting more tailgaters, smiling, shaking hands, hugging fans, thanking them and promising them that his team would give their best effort later in the day, all to reward them for their support. He even sat in a fan's zero-gravity recliner, relishing his interaction, soaking in the moment, savoring it, understanding that this was what made college football—and his job—so spine-tingling wonderful. He estimated that there must have been fifteen thousand fans already outside the stadium.

When he returned to the hotel, he told his players about what he had witnessed and that this was what made Clemson special. This was quintessential Dabo, the ultimate people person, doing what he did best off the field: making strangers feel like his friends—and making them feel like they were vital parts of his team.

Clemson won the game 42–36 on a 31-yard touchdown pass from Watson to Jordan Leggett with 3:14 remaining in the fourth quarter. Louisville reached the Tigers' 9-yard line with less than a minute to play, but on fourth-and-twelve, Lamar Jackson completed a pass to James Quick, who was pushed out of bounds one-yard short of the first-down marker. Thousands and thousands of Clemson fans—perhaps some of the same fans that Dabo had pressed flesh with ten hours earlier—poured onto the field after the final whistle blew.

CLEMSON WASN'T PERFECT IN 2016, however. On November 12, at home in Memorial Stadium, Pittsburgh kicker Chris Blewitt—who definitely didn't *blow it* late in the game—hit a 48-yard field goal with six seconds remaining in the fourth quarter to lift the Panthers over the Tigers 43–42. Clemson's defense had sleepwalked through most of the sixty minutes of action, and the Tigers, who had entered the game ranked second in the College Football Playoff standings, lost to an unranked opponent for the first time in forty-six games. "Prosperity is a terrible teacher," Dabo said a few days later.

But the loss did have a positive effect: It awoke a somnolent football beast. Clemson won its next two games by an average of 45.5 points and then beat Virginia Tech for the ACC championship, 42–35. The Tigers regained their No. 2 spot in the final college football rankings and earned their second straight playoff bid.

For their national semifinal game, the Tigers returned to the Arizona desert to face Ohio State. Dabo told his players that they could begin to wash away the pain of last year's defeat to Alabama in Glendale if they could celebrate with a win over the Buckeyes. The Tigers' performance was ruthless: Clemson demolished Ohio State 31–0, the first time in 194 games a team coached by Urban Meyer had ever been shut out. Top-ranked Alabama also won its national semifinal game over Washington, setting the stage for a rematch of the previous year's title game between the two teams that began the season ranked numbers one and two.

"If you're going to be the best," Dabo said of Alabama, "you've got to beat them."

TWO DAYS BEFORE THE national title game, Dabo met with the media. Many coaches act like they'd rather watch paint dry or be at an aluminum-siding convention rather than take questions from reporters, but not Dabo, who typically enjoys his time in front of the camera and uses those occasions to send messages to his players and the Clemson fan base. His natural-born talent for storytelling—a skill he inherited from his late father—had served him well throughout his career, and it did again forty-eight hours before his team played in the game that was called Clemson–Alabama Part Two.

A reporter asked Dabo what a win over the Crimson Tide would mean for his program. Dabo articulated a long-winded response about giving underdogs everywhere a sense of hope and that it would send a message that anything is possible. He then mentioned a question that had been frequently asked around the Clemson football offices since he had ascended to the head coaching position eight years earlier.

He asked the media, How do you eat an elephant?

He waited one beat, two—giving his astute audience a chance to realize that the mascot of the Alabama Crimson Tide, the team that had dominated college football for the better part of a decade, is an elephant.

"One bite at a time," he said. "One bite at a time."

The lesson here: You beat Alabama by having each player on your team focus on winning his one-on-one battle against the Tide player lined up in front of him, and do that one play at a time, throughout every play of the entire game. You do your job on every snap and don't worry about how your teammates are doing. You channel all of your energy on what is directly in front of you.

It was a metaphor that could have described "The Process," Saban's coaching philosophy. Ever since Saban had asked Dabo to be an assistant on his first staff in Tuscaloosa in 2007, Dabo had studied Saban, determining and dissecting and replicating the steps he had taken to win national title after national title. Dabo learned that Alabama's coach was a master at managing his staff. He was wasn't afraid to change his offensive or defensive schemes, he was obsessively detailed and committed to recruiting—and, with a few carefully chosen words, he could inspire his players to play at their peak.

Dabo had spent the previous few years mimicking Saban, so much so that the Tiger staff began calling themselves—in private—the Clemson Tide. Like Saban, Dabo clearly defined the roles of everyone on his staff and, much like Saban, Dabo hired coaches who were ambitious and aspired to one day become head coaches. That meant they were hungry—willing to log long hours when necessary and wanting success at every turn. To both Saban and Dabo, work ethic mattered more than work experience. And like Saban, Dabo hadn't been afraid to fire key personnel if they didn't get the job done (see Kevin Steele).

And also like Saban, Dabo had altered his scheme when he had hired Chad Morris to be his offensive coordinator in 2011 and installed a smashmouth spread attack in favor of a traditional set. He updated his recruiting war room so that it resembled the one in Tuscaloosa. He had his assistants devote at least some time to recruiting every working day of the year, precisely what Saban had instituted at Alabama. And like Saban, Dabo had become a savant at inspiring his players— a skill that Dabo would lean on when it mattered most in the upcoming national title game.

THE TIDE ENTERED RAYMOND James Stadium in Tampa on a twenty-six-game winning streak. Saban was 5-0 in national championship games and most sports books in Las Vegas listed Alabama as a 6.5-point favorite. Yet Dabo oozed confidence in the locker room before kickoff, turning his pregame speech into a sermon on expectations. "When we win this game tonight, I don't want to hear one word about this being an upset," Dabo told his players. "The only upset is going to be if we don't win the dadgum game."

On an unseasonably cool Florida night, Clemson trailed 14–7 at the end of the second quarter. As he eyed his players in the locker room during the halftime break, Dabo remembered the word he had chosen as the theme for his season: love. He yelled out to Jay Guillermo, the Tigers' starting center.

"Jay, you love Deshaun, right?"

"Yes, sir," Guillermo replied.

"Deshaun," he said, "you love when [senior running back] Wayne Gallman lines up behind you, right?"

"Yes, sir."

Swinney did this with a few more players, reminding them of the bond they had with each other, the hours and hours of work they had put in together to reach this moment, and the pure love they felt for each other. "Guys, we know we're good enough to win this game," he said. "We got this far because we love each other. Let's just go out there and finish it."

With 2:07 to play in the fourth quarter, Alabama quarterback Jalen Hurts galloped through the Clemson defense on a 30-yard scoring run, giving the Tide a 31–28 lead. As soon as Hurts reached the end zone, Deshaun Watson, who had been sitting on a folding chair on the sideline, immediately stood up and turned his eyes to the scoreboard to see how much time was left. There was no hint of a here-we-go-again demeanor projected by Clemson's quarterback, only determination. The previous January, Watson felt like he had just run out of time against Alabama. His eyes still locked on the clock, Watson smiled.

On the sideline, Dabo gathered his team and staff. He pointed to the scoreboard that read 31–28 and yelled, "Can you believe this? Isn't this fun?"

Once in the huddle to start the final drive of the night at Clemson's 32-yard line, Watson told his teammates, "Let's be legendary," sounding very much like his head coach. Watson then calmly led his team down the field, featuring passes of 24 yards to Mike Williams and 17 yards to Jordan Leggett. With six seconds on the clock, Clemson faced a first and goal at the Alabama 2-yard line.

The play was called Orange Crush, and it featured an outside receiver on the right side of the field running a slant route to the inside that could prevent an opposing defensive back from following the inside receiver on the right side running an out route toward the sideline. The Tiger staff hadn't run this crossing routes play the entire postseason, waiting for the perfect moment to call it. Now that moment had arrived.

Former walk-on senior wide receiver Hunter Renfrow lined up as the inside receiver on the right side. Renfrow had already caught nine passes, even though he looked more like a kicker than a wide receiver. Generously listed at 5'11" and 180 pounds, he was the son of a coach. The previous year in the national title game, Renfrow had caught a then career-high seven passes for 88 yards and two touchdowns. Throw in his receding hairline and his small hands, and he hardly looked like an Alabama killer, which soon would become his nickname. From the first time he saw him play, Dabo loved his grit.

After the snap of the ball, Renfrow broke free through traffic in the secondary on an out route. Watson rolled to his right and tossed the ball. Renfrow was wide open. He cradled the ball in his arms, scoring with one second remaining on the clock. Alabama coaches yelled for a flag, believing that cornerback Marlon Humphrey had been illegally picked on the play, but the referees shook their heads. The touchdown stood. The Tigers had consumed the elephant, with one, final succulent bite.

AS SOON AS IT was over, Dabo ran onto the field with his entire team, overjoyed. Kathleen, dressed in an orange skirt and jacket, weaved her way through the frenzied crowd and reached her husband near midfield. She wrapped her arms around him, holding him tight, as a Clemson player dumped Gatorade on the two of them, the first couple of Tiger football.

Saban, surrounded by state troopers, searched for Dabo amid the chaos and finally found him, shaking his hand and congratulating him. This was a handshake that Dabo had been waiting for since he was a boy listening to Alabama games crackle on the radio. After exchanging a few words with Saban and giving him a pat on the back, Dabo then climbed onto a makeshift stage that had been pulled onto the field.

Dabo's mom, Carol, found her son on the stage and told him she loved him. For a moment, time froze. The mother looked at her son, remembered him as a little boy, thought about the tough times, the nights they stayed together in the same bed while living together in Tuscaloosa, and all the hard work that her Dabo had put in that led to this crowning hour. As she looked at the trophy and gazed at her boy, she couldn't have been more proud.

It was nearing 1:00 a.m. local time when Dabo, onstage, grabbed a microphone and spoke to the thousands of Clemson fans still in the stands, not wanting the night to end, waiting for their Southern preacher to speak to their congregation of true believers. "I knew they wouldn't quit," he said of his players. "I talked to them about letting the light inside of them always be brighter than the light that's shining on them. If they focused on that, they'd be OK."

Dabo then talked about his personal journey, about being hired eight years earlier and the plan he had for constructing a national champion. During the season, Clemson had beaten the last seven national champions. "At the top of the mountain, that Clemson flag is flying!" he said to his adoring masses, and then he lifted the trophy up to the heavens.

AT ABOUT 2:00 A.M. local time, Dabo embraced his family again and told his mom, "I gotta take a shower. Tell the bus not to leave me."

After cleaning himself up, Dabo put on a blazer and orange necktie. He emerged from the locker room and walked side by side with his wife toward the ten idling buses parked outside the stadium. As he neared Bus 1 to take his normal spot in

Seat 1, Row 1, he spotted a handful of Clemson fans who were waiting to catch one last glimpse of their coach. Dabo yelled, "I'll see y'all in Death Valley!"

Dabo and Kathleen stepped on board the bus. Several of the players and their family members had fallen asleep— it was now nearing 2:30 a.m.—but Dabo wasn't about to let the moment pass without reminding them of what they just accomplished. "Hey!" Dabo yelled, startling several dozing players. "I don't know if y'all heard, but this bus is only supposed to be used by the national champions. So...I guess this is our bus." The suddenly awake players whooped and cheered and hollered.

Led by police motorcycles, their blue and red lights penetrating the darkness, ten team buses carrying the exhilarated but exhausted national champions rolled into the cool South Florida night, the last stretch for a team on the ride of their lives.

CHAPTER 10

EXTRAVAGANT DREAMING

The cavalcade of convertibles and orange jeeps rolled down College Avenue five days after Clemson had knocked off Alabama 35–31. Dabo and his family rode in a classic blue Cadillac roadster on this cool winter afternoon, waving to adoring fans that lined the street three- and four-deep in downtown Clemson. Tiger Nation showered the players and Swinneys with love and reverence as they made their way toward Memorial Stadium. The victory parade was years in the making, and it had a Caesar-returning-to-Rome feel—the only thing missing were garlands and chariots.

The previous year, Dabo and the Tiger staff had held a pizza party at Memorial Stadium to watch the College Football Play-off Selection Show. More than thirty thousand fans showed up and screamed in ecstasy when Clemson was tabbed the top seed. Now, on January 14, 2017, more than sixty-five thousand filled the stadium at the end of the parade route.

Once out of the blue Caddy, Dabo climbed the steps onto a makeshift stage erected in the east end zone and took a seat in the front row, his players flanking around and behind him. Nearly ninety minutes would pass before Dabo, wearing a light brown pinstriped suit, rose to address the crowd. Within seconds, a still hush enveloped the entire stadium, his voice quieting the expectant gathering. He spoke for just thirty minutes, but in that time he provided a detailed, step-by-step review of how the program was built during the eight years of his tenure and why it would flourish in the future. His eyes squinted and became slightly teary when he thanked those who believed in him, especially former athletic director Terry Don Phillips, who took a chance on the young wide receivers coach back in 2008.

"There's not a lot of people in this world who have the guts and conviction to do what they believe regardless of what other people think," Dabo said. "Terry Don Phillips, he's one of them."

Near the end of his speech, Dabo talked about dreaming, a subject the former walk-on at Alabama knew well. "Greatness is for all of us," he said. "If you truly believe, you can do anything. You can dream big, man. I'm talking about extravagant dreaming."

Extravagant dreaming. Now, that was a phrase that described the Tao of Dabo as well as any.

THAT SAME MONTH—JANUARY 2017—the Allen N. Reeves Football Complex opened for business. It was the Taj Mahal of football, a 142,500-square-foot facility that cost at least $55 million to build. Its features included an indoor practice facility and practice fields, a grand lobby that housed national championship trophies, a bowling alley, an arcade, a barbershop, a sauna, a sixty-person cold tub, a virtual-reality room, and a nap room. Plus a far-as-the-eye-could-see dining hall with a biometric scanner to help players monitor nutrition, and a 23,000-square-foot weight room that could turn any ninety-pound weakling into a championship body builder. Dabo even put in a slide to provide a fun way to move from the second floor to ground level, the idea coming to him after he saw the 2013 movie *The Internship* and noted the slide in Google's headquarters. He thought it was so cool that he ordered a stainless-steel slide and arranged it so it ran from outside the coaches' offices on the second floor down to the first, where it spit riders out near the team's locker rooms and weight room. It was dubbed the "Dabo slide." To open spring practice in 2017, Dabo—his eyes wide with a gleeful smile—glided down the slide like a kid at recess.

Outside the complex, known as the "Players Village," there is a Wiffle Ball diamond with artificial turf, a sand volleyball court, a nine-hole miniature golf course, a regulation-sized basketball court, a horseshoe pit, and a covered four-season pavilion that has a fire pit. The whole facility screamed fun; the whole facility screamed Dabo, who had a hand in designing every aspect of the structure. The audacity of the project reflected Dabo's expanding dreams at Clemson; frontiers of possibility that had once seemed so far away were now in his rearview mirror.

"The mindset of this building has always been about the players," said Thad Turnipseed. "Dabo told us, 'Make it Clemson.' And Clemson is family and fun."

FIVE MONTHS AFTER WINNING the school's first national championship in thirty-five years, Clemson players and coaches descended on the White House to be greeted by President Donald Trump. Many of the players and coaches wore their national championship rings, which included a depiction of a tiger climbing a mountain and the words *A little bit more.*

After the president said a few remarks to the team on a sun-splashed afternoon on the South Lawn, Dabo gave an eight-minute speech that outlined the core values of his program and what pushed him to succeed. It was as much a blueprint of his philosophy about life as it was a speech about his team. "Life is truly about how we live between the [special] moments," he said as the president stood close by. "That's really what it comes down to. It's all about how we live between the moments. It's treating others the right way. It's random acts of kindness. It's just doing the little things in a great way."

He glanced at his players standing behind him. "If you take anything else from this past season, you saw what can happen when you really put your heart into something. It's always about what's next. The best is truly yet to come. I love all of you. This is something that we all dreamed about."

Here was Dabo again emphasizing *love*. If there was one lesson he wanted his players to take away from the season, it was the power of love and what can happen when you live by the very meaning and spirit of that word.

THE TOP COACHES IN all sports are always searching for an edge over the competition—what it will take to beat their opponents. Studying the science of sleep for college football players was an emerging trend in the late 2010s, and Dabo made sure that his program stayed on the cutting edge.

After winning the national title, Dabo and the Clemson staff provided an application to players to download onto their smartphones so they could monitor their sleep patterns. Alabama's players used an app called Rise, and if there was one way to prod Dabo to do something, it was to inform him that Alabama was doing it. Yet Dabo had long believed that one of the biggest issues facing college football players was their lack of quality sleep—the other was the issue of mental health—and so he was in favor of this from the start.

Starting at the beginning of the 2017 season, Clemson partnered with Rise Science, a Chicago-based company that essentially conducted a large-scale sleep study of the players, examining how their sleep habits translated to performance on the field, in the weight room, and in meetings with coaches and support staff. At first, thirty-five players participated. Small, leather sensors, placed under their beds, monitored the length and quality of their sleep every night. The following mornings, the coaches received an email that included a minute-by-minute report featuring charts and statistics about how the player slept. The staff could see how many hours of sleep a player averaged per night over a week and a month, how often their sleep was considered "restless," what their heart rate was when they slept, and how much the rate changed throughout each night. Armed with this information, the Clemson staff could develop a specific plan for each player to maximize the quality of their sleep.

If a player struggled to sleep well, for example, he might be given a pair of orange-lens glasses to wear to bed. They blocked out blue light and helped the brain produce melatonin, a hormone made by the pineal gland—a pea-sized gland located above the middle of the brain—that helps the body know when it is time to go to sleep. Players were told not to play video games thirty minutes before lying down for the night, because the stimulation the games caused often delay falling asleep for thirty minutes or more.

The output of the sensors also pointed to players who suffered stress and may be on the verge of a mental health condition. In such cases, Dabo and staff held one-on-one discussions with the affected players and helped them overcome the impediments to sound health.

ON JANUARY 1, 2018, Clemson faced Alabama in the College Football Playoffs for the third consecutive season. Round Three took place in the national semifinals in New Orleans. The Superdome in the Big Easy was a special place for Dabo: It was the site of his greatest victory as a player at Alabama, when the Tide defeated the Miami Hurricanes 34–13 in the Sugar Bowl to win the 1992 national title.

The last time Dabo had been in the Superdome was a year earlier, in December 2016, when he and Deshaun Watson traveled to New Orleans for the Manning Award presentation. Dabo took his quarterback on a quick tour of the Dome, telling him stories of that night when the Crimson Tide toppled the Hurricanes, how that was his final game as a player, how special it was to stand on the sideline in the waning moments of the fourth quarter knowing that he and his teammates were about to be crowned champions. Just like when he was a player, Dabo took several pictures of his time in the Superdome with Watson. It was good to be back, and let loose so many good reminders of why Dabo loved the game so much. In the history of the sport, what other former walk-on wide receiver ever stole the game ball from an equipment manager and ran around the field after a national championship victory-slapping hands with fans?

In the days leading up to the semifinal game against Bama, reporters frequently asked Dabo about the twenty-fifth anniversary of that game. Earlier in the season, Dabo had returned to Tuscaloosa for a reunion of that team. On October 13, 2017, Clemson lost to Syracuse 27–24 in the Carrier Dome in upstate New York on a Friday night. In spite of his disappointment, Dabo walked over to the Syracuse locker room after the game and spoke to the Orange players, telling them how impressed he was with their play and that what they did was no fluke. He then traveled with his team back to Clemson, arriving at 5:00 a.m. Then, after a brief rest, he flew to Tuscaloosa for the reunion, an event he wasn't going to miss, sleep or no sleep.

"When we get together we all slip back into our old roles and it's like time has stood still," said Antonio Langham, a cornerback on that '92 team. "We cut up on Dabo like he was the walk-on and scout team player he used to be."

Before Alabama faced Arkansas at Bryant–Denny Stadium that evening, the players from the '92 squad were introduced to the crowd. Dabo waved and flashed his Huck Finn grin as the fans exploded in a frenzy when his image appeared on the big screen, a returning hero who many in attendance believed would one day come home to Alabama and be the coach of the Tide. Dabo could have easily skipped the event— his mind was racing with all that had gone wrong at Syracuse less than twenty-four hours earlier—but it was important to him to be back with his teammates, his best friends, his guys. It all reminded him of his halcyon days in Tuscaloosa. He must have hugged every former teammate.

Dabo left soon after kickoff and was back in his office by halftime. He had work to do, problems to solve. But what a wonderful quick trip down memory lane it had been, losing himself in the nostalgia and joy of having been a Crimson Tide football player—and a national champion.

AFTER LOSING TO SYRACUSE on a rare Friday night game, Clemson won five straight to advance to the ACC title game, where the Tigers faced Miami. Before the game, Dabo had a

long talk his quarterback Kelly Bryant, who all season long
was dogged with questions by reporters about the difficulty
of replacing a legend like Deshaun Watson, who had been
a first-round draft pick by the Houston Texans the previous
April. Dabo told his junior signal-caller that he "needed to be
the best version of Kelly B you can be." On this chilly night
in Charlotte, Bryant was: He started the game by completing
a championship-game record fifteen straight passes. Bryant
was named the MVP after throwing for 252 yards and scoring
two touchdowns in Clemson's 38–3 victory.

The Tigers earned the top seed in the College Football
Playoffs, which meant that Dabo got to pick where his team
would play its national semifinal game. The choice was easy:
the Superdome in New Orleans, the site of Dabo's greatest triumph as a player twenty-five years earlier. "We're the
attacking champs," Dabo said. "We're attacking to try to win
another one."

Next up: Alabama (again).

THE THIRD EPISODE OF the trilogy wasn't close: Fourth-ranked
Alabama dominated No. 1 Clemson from the opening kickoff
in the Sugar Bowl, when Crimson Tide cornerback Trevon
Diggs unloaded a devastating hit on Tiger running back Travis
Etienne. The Tide defense was ruthless, forcing Clemson
into three straight three-and-outs to start the game and held
the Tigers' offense to 261 total yards. Bryant was ineffective
against a vicious Alabama pass rush. The Tigers lost 24–6.

"I tell our guys all the time, it's always about what's

next," Dabo said after the game. "We're going to learn and we're going to grow and we're going to always get better. My expectation is to be right back here next year, right back in the middle of it, right back in the thick of it...I don't think this will be the last one....We'll be back and so will they. We'll have probably several more opportunities to hook it up with these guys. And we look forward to that."

Dabo later shared a graphic metaphor with his players about their underachieving performance in the game—a visual that was about as R-rated as Dabo was capable of producing. According to defensive lineman Clelin Ferrell (another future NFL first-round draft pick), Dabo remarked about the 24–6 loss: "He said... 'That's kind of like going to the bathroom and taking a dump. You got the job done, but you guys didn't wipe. And when you don't wipe, it's like you didn't finish.'"

The lack of a downfield passing game against Alabama in the national semifinals of the 2017 College Football Playoff loss had been the team's fatal flaw. But a few days after the defeat, a quarterback named Trevor Lawrence enrolled at Clemson in early January 2018. He broke all of Watson's high school records in the state of Georgia, playing at Cartersville, a suburb of northwest Atlanta. Dabo couldn't hide his giddiness on the day that Lawrence signed his letter of intent. "He's just so physically developed for a young guy," Dabo said. "Deshaun was obviously pretty special coming out of Georgia. He's just way ahead of Deshaun from a physical standpoint....He's got everything that you look for, that you could possibly want. He's just been a natural from day one, all the way from ninth grade."

The rearming of Clemson football was underway.

DABO TYPICALLY EXUDES A nice-guy, Mr. Rogers aura, but like any successful head coach or leader, he's not shy about making difficult, cutthroat decisions. Remember those frenzied, frenetic first hours when he was named interim head coach back in 2008? He made the difficult call to fire offensive coordinator Rob Spence and install himself and twenty-nine-year-old assistant Billy Napier as the offensive play callers. Two years later, he canned Napier and hired Tulsa offensive coordinator Chad Morris, who was only one year removed from coaching high school ball in Texas. Or a year later when he axed defensive coordinator Kevin Steele after the Tigers surrendered 70 points to West Virginia in the Orange Bowl. Dabo doesn't covet hard choices, but he will always do what he believes is best for the team—a lesson learned up close and personal when Tommy Bowden abruptly resigned in 2008 because he believed he had become a distraction to the program.

Now in the summer and fall of 2018, Dabo had another tough call to make: Who should he start at quarterback, the veteran Kelly Bryant or the uniquely talented freshman Trevor Lawrence? The loss to Alabama in the Sugar Bowl the previous January had exposed Bryant's limitations as a passer. Dabo opted to hold an open competition in summer camp, and he decided to start Bryant and play Lawrence in a few series each game, testing whether his freshman was ready to play big-time college football. In the game against Georgia Tech on September 22, Bryant struggled with his throws and decision-making. The planned platoon system didn't last long: Lawrence ascended to the job, completing thirteen of eighteen for 176 yards and four touchdowns as Clemson went on to win 49–21 over the Yellow Jackets. Following the game, Dabo named Lawrence the starter.

Dabo allowed Bryant to miss practice the next Monday to digest the demotion. Then Bryant failed to attend Tuesday's practice. He ultimately transferred to Missouri. When news leaked that Bryant had quit the team, senior defensive tackle Christian Wilkins took Lawrence to breakfast at Clemson's SunnySide Cafe. The team's most respected player, Wilkins told Lawrence he had the full support of every player. This act of taking his young quarterback to breakfast was why character matters to Dabo—and why he preaches the virtues of leadership to his seniors. What could have been a very divisive situation—Bryant had many friends on the team—turned out to be a transformative one.

THE FIRST START OF Trevor Lawrence's college career was not a masterpiece. Playing at home against Syracuse on September 29, 2018, the Tigers fell behind 6–0. Then, midway through the first quarter, Lawrence led a 60-yard drive that culminated with a 1-yard touchdown run by sophomore running back Travis Etienne, giving the Tigers a 7–6 lead. A four-star recruit, Etienne had gained a total of 8,864 yards and scored a hard-to-fathom 115 touchdowns at Jennings High School in

Jennings, Louisiana, located about ninety miles from the LSU campus. Ed Orgeron, long known as one of the top recruiters in college football, desperately tried to convince Etienne to play for his home-state Tigers, emphasizing LSU tradition of putting running backs into the NFL, from Leonard Fournette to Kevin Faulk to former Heisman winner Billy Cannon.

But Etienne—who would go on to become a two-time ACC player of the year and set the Football Bowl Subdivision (FBS) record for scoring a touchdown in forty-six career games—spurned LSU for Clemson. "I'm sick to my stomach," said Orgeron, who became the Tigers' head coach in 2016 after being the team's recruiting coordinator and defensive line coach. "We wanted Etienne." But he signed with Clemson for one reason: the connection he felt with entire staff, especially offensive coordinator Tony Elliott.

On a Friday night before a game in 2016, Elliott was DM'ing with Etienne as Elliott sat in a movie theater with the rest of the team, trying to convince the running back to come to Clemson. Four days later, Elliott was face-to-face with the running back in his hometown, securing Etienne's commitment. The pursuit of Etienne illustrated once again Clemson's relentless, every-single-day dedication to recruiting.

Against Syracuse, Etienne carried the ball twenty-seven times for 203 yards and scored three touchdowns—just another day on the field for the 5'10", 205-pound back. The Tigers won 27–23 in what would be their closest game of the regular season. Clemson won their fourth consecutive ACC title by defeating Pittsburgh 42–10 in the conference championship game—Lawrence threw for 327 yards and three touchdowns—and finished the regular season ranked No. 2 in the College Football Playoff rankings. In their semifinal against Notre Dame in the Cotton Bowl, the Tigers seized the lead late in the second quarter when Lawrence hit wide receiver Justyn Ross on a 52-yard scoring pass, pushing the score to 9–3.

The route was just beginning as Clemson won 30–3, the gap in talent between the rosters as wide as the Grand Canyon, with the Tigers outgaining the Irish 538 yards to 248. "They were the better team," Irish coach Brian Kelly said. "There's no doubt about that."

ON JANUARY 7, 2019, Clemson squared off against Alabama in the playoffs for the fourth straight year. In his pregame press conference before the national championship game in Santa Clara, California, Dabo spoke in wonderment of being in the shadow of San Francisco, playing up the role of a country rube visiting a big city out west for the first time.

"I just saw my first tumbleweed," he said. "I've never seen a tumbleweed in my entire life. We don't have tumbleweeds in Alabama or South Carolina. We're coming down the road on a bus, and this huge, like, ball of sticks, that's the only way I can [describe it]—just comes right at the bus. I'm like, what the heck is that? [The bus driver is] like, 'That's a tumble-weed.' I thought those were just in like Roadrunner or the movies or something."

Was this an act, a coach hoping to suppress expectations by acting like he was completely out of his element? Or was

this Dabo just being Dabo, articulating his genuine amaze-
ment at seeing something he'd never laid eyes on before? To
those who know him the best, the answer was obvious: This
was quintessential Dabo, who is curious about everything
and will talk about anything—usually with a country-boy,
holy-cow grin on his face. To the local California media, it
was catnip, prompting more than a few stories about Dabo's
Southern roots.

On the eve of the game, Dabo reflected to a group of
reporters on how far his program had come.

When I got the job in 2009, I felt like at Clemson we
could build a program that could compete at the highest
level. We were a long way from that. That's for sure. But
I felt like we had a few pieces in place and we just needed
to build an infrastructure, we needed to modernize our
program in every sense of the word, from staff to our
recruiting to our facilities to the way the administration
thought. You name it.

But for me, I felt like we needed to play a tough
schedule...You can't be afraid to fall, all right. There's
going to be some failure. But that's a part of your growth.
That's a part of development. That's the only way I'm
going to be able to teach these guys what it takes. So
from day one, we've played Georgia, played Auburn four
times. We've played Texas A&M, Notre Dame, LSU, we've
played a lot of people in and outside of our conference
that allowed us to compete and develop the program to

where we could match up and have the type of postseason success we've had over the past five or six years.

Dabo then spoke of Nick Saban and how for years he'd been studying what Saban had been in doing in Tuscaloosa.

From a program standpoint, when Coach Saban got to Alabama, how he modernized the program, infrastructure-wise, to create an environment that's conducive to helping the young players have a great experience and to develop as a person and a player. And there are resources involved with that, and I think that's something that Coach Saban changed in college football, quite frankly.

When I was an assistant, when he became the head coach and started putting that in place, it was something that I paid attention to, because the old model where you had the head coach and nine assistants and a couple GA's and you were everything: you were the coach, you were the counselor, you wore every hat. In the meantime, recruiting is still going on, problems happen, these kids are kids and they have family issues.

As a coach, we're always studying and trying to learn from every program, and Alabama has certainly been the standard for a decade or so since he's been there. So I've learned lots of things. Sometimes it could just be maybe how he handles a situation. I've called on him a time or two to ask him his opinion on some things and we've swapped some ideas. I'm thankful that I've been able to learn…There are a lot of similarities [between our programs], yet personality-wise maybe we're different in how we go about certain things.

ALABAMA HAD WON FIVE of the previous nine national championships. But almost from the opening whistle, the Tide committed one mistake after another: Alabama quarterback Tua Tagovailoa threw an interception on the Tide's third offensive snap, which A.J. Terrell returned for a 44-yard touchdown; Alabama committed uncharacteristic penalties, consistently failed to line up correctly on defense, and suffered special teams gaffes. It was a nightmare game for Saban and a too-good-to-be-true night for Dabo. Clemson won 44–16, Saban's most lopsided loss in his tenure at Tuscaloosa. Trevor Lawrence—who threw for 347 yards and three touchdowns—became the first true freshman to start and win a national championship game since Jamelle Holieway led Oklahoma to a 20–10 victory over Penn State on January 1, 1986. With the victory, Clemson became the first team in 121 seasons to go 15-0.

Dabo was so caught up in the excitement that, after Alabama's final offensive possession—after Clemson's Christian Wilkins and Xavier Thomas tackled quarterback Jalen Hurts for a 4-yard loss—the coach raced down the sideline at near full sprint and collided with junior defensive end Clelin Ferrell for a midair hip bump. This was not a typical move by a head coach, but Dabo couldn't contain his emotions. He had won a national title before, but never with such a beautifully efficient and overwhelming performance as this.

After the blowout, as Dabo walked through the darkened halls of Levi's Stadium, he spoke about why his team had won its second national title in three years. "To be successful, you have to have a vision for what you want to do and a clear plan," he said. "And then you can't be afraid to fail. You've got to keep getting up. That's what we've done for ten years."

Late in the night, about two hours after the victory, Dabo hugged his family outside the Clemson locker room. The players and coaches were already on the team buses, but Dabo wasn't ready to leave, not yet, not before savoring and lingering in the moment a little longer. So Dabo guided his wife and other family members back onto the Levi's Stadium field. The stands were empty and now, together in the cool California night, the Swinney family dropped to the grass and made snow angels in the purple and orange confetti that earlier had been shot out of cannons and floated onto the field. It was a heartwarming scene, this moment of the family celebrating together, the portraits of childlike joy etched on every face in the Swinney brood.

DABO AND NICK SABAN typically spent their summer vacations in the same town: Boca Grande, Florida, which sits on Gasparilla Island, a barrier island in the Gulf of Mexico off the southwest coast of Florida. The island is about seven miles long and one mile wide. There are no traffic lights, buildings can't be taller than three stories, there are no chain stores, and it has a population of about seventeen hundred. It's known for its pristine, white-sand beaches and its deep-sea fishing. The *Wall Street Journal* once selected the island as one of the ten best places in the country to own a second home.

Residents and visitors to the island tend to leave Saban and Dabo alone as they drive their golf carts—the primary mode of transportation on the island—to the beach or to restaurants. Dabo started vacationing on Gasparilla around 1994, when he was a graduate assistant at Alabama. He and his wife fell in love with the place and returned often. In 2010, after Dabo's salary jumped to $800,000 a year, the Swinneys purchased their own home in Boca Grande. A few years later, Saban bought a house on the island. They both said it was a coincidence that they ended up buying second homes on the same small strip off the Gulf Coast, but coaches tend to talk about vacation plans and where they can go to disappear, so it's not surprising that they wound up with homes about five miles apart. And because most college football coaches have similar summer schedules, the two started bumping into each other on Gasparilla once the Sabans rolled into Boca Grande.

The Swinneys live near the south end, which is closer to the town shops and restaurants. They enjoy going to Sisters Restaurant, and they have a tricked out, fully loaded pontoon boat, which Dabo pilots into the green-and-aqua Gulf waters. The Swinneys have been known to throw blowout Fourth of July parties that feature a taco truck, an ice cream truck, and a karaoke machine that stays fired up for hours. "I've kind of got my own little world down there," Dabo said. "It's just quiet, nobody's there. Then all crap breaks loose [when I get back]."

The Sabans' beach house is in a quieter neighborhood on the north end of the island. "Dabo is better than Nick at disconnecting [in Boca Grande]," said Thad Turnipseed, who has worked for both coaches. "Nick is good but when Dabo is down there those three weeks, football is the last thing on his mind. Nick might drag it up, but Dabo would cut it off quick. He respects the way we do it [at Clemson] and he knows they're different. But they're close enough that they can kid each other about that."

Every so often, Saban and Dabo have socialized. They've played golf together, gone for boat rides, had dinner, and developed a genuine friendship—something especially rare for Saban, whose circle of close friends can be counted on two hands. "The situation sort of offers us the opportunity to get together sometimes and talk about things," Saban said in 2017. "And we do a lot."

Before Clemson and Alabama played in the national championship game in 2016, Saban called Dabo and made him a bet: The loser had to buy the winner a dinner of his choice at a restaurant in Boca Grande called The Temptation, which is known for its soft-shell crab, fried oysters, and ribeye steaks with Andouille gravy. Clemson lost the game, and Dabo sent Saban a $250 gift certificate. On the bottom of the certificate Dabo wrote: "C.U. in Tampa next year!"

The following year, as Dabo had prophesied, the two teams clashed again for the national title in Tampa. This time Clemson won on a last-second touchdown and Saban—never one to lose an opportunity to establish his position of power in a relationship—doubled the amount that Dabo had spent on him and sent Dabo a $500 gift certificate to The Temptation.

Saban mailed Dabo another $500 gift certificate to The Temp after the Tigers beat the Crimson Tide 44–16 in January 2019. That summer, Dabo, gift certificate in hand, took his family to the restaurant. After their meal was over, a co-owner of The Temp, Kevin Stockdale, approached the Swinneys. He asked Dabo if his meal was to his liking.

"Kevin," Dabo said, "that was the best meal I've ever had."

At that instant, Dabo looked like the most fulfilled, satisfied man Stockdale had ever seen. He understood why:

That victory meal had been courtesy of one Nick Saban.

CHAPTER 11

THE FUTURE OF LITTLE OL' CLEMSON

During the 2019 season, as the Tigers were aiming for their third national title in four years, Dabo injected a woebegone phrase into the national sports conversation: "Little Ol' Clemson."

Over the course of Clemson's steady rise in the nation's football consciousness through the previous decade, the Tigers had never seized the country's imagination the way Alabama, Ohio State, University of Southern California, Texas, or even Nebraska did in their trophy-winning heydays. These traditional powers of college football had fan bases that stretched from coast to coast, from Dallas to the Dakotas, consistently drawing huge television audiences and revenues. But that wasn't the case with Clemson. Even though the Tigers had indeed reached the zenith of the sport, Clemson didn't possess the mystique and intrigue of programs that were nowhere near their equal on the field. The question was: Why?

The Future of Little Ol' Clemson

At the midpoint of the 2019 season, Dabo expressed utter dismay when his team was dropped from preseason No. 1 in the AP poll to No. 3 without losing a single game. He understood that the ACC wasn't highly regarded by AP voters—the conference had only one other team, Virginia, in the Top 25 and the Cavaliers were far from being a playoff title contender. Each team in the SEC played a Murderers' Row of a schedule every season—other than Vanderbilt, there were no perennial cupcakes to feast on in that conference—and the Big 10 and Big 12 each annually featured at least three teams that appeared capable of reaching the playoffs. But the ACC? For several years, Clemson operated in its own stratosphere and faced few serious threats to their conference hegemony, which made their path to the College Football Playoffs far easier than the likes of Alabama, Ohio State, and Oklahoma.

Nonetheless, Dabo believed Clemson wasn't getting the recognition and acclaim its performances on the field deserved. As a former longshot walk-on at Alabama, Dabo always relished playing the disrespect card. And now he leaned on that underdog mentality again when he introduced into the lexicon the phrase "Little Ol' Clemson."

But just because Dabo was at "Little Ol' Clemson" didn't mean his influence in college football was diminished. One story illustrated the essential meaning of Dabo for up-and-coming coaches: One afternoon early in the summer of 2016, Will Healy, who was then in his first year as head coach at Austin Peay State University, was driving through the Alabama countryside on a recruiting mission when his phone rang. The caller ID revealed the number was in South Carolina. Healey had no idea who the caller was, but, curious, he said, "Hello?"

"Hey, this is Dabo Swinney," the voice told a stunned Healy, who had never met Dabo.

Dabo proceeded to lobby Healy to hire one of his graduate assistants. Healy was in awe, because Dabo was his favorite coach. He loved how Dabo interacted with his players and how much he appeared to enjoy himself on the sideline whenever he saw him on television. To Healy, Dabo made coaching fun again. Near the end of their conversation, Healy couldn't help but gush: "You don't know me from Adam. But I just want to say thank you for what you've done for this profession, because the people getting in it now know you can do things the way you [do]...and still have success."

And just because Dabo called his school "Little Ol' Clemson" that didn't stop the Tiger athletic administration in April 2019 from rewarding Dabo the biggest contract in college football history. The contract, a ten-year, $93 million deal that would keep Dabo at Clemson through the 2028 season, included an unusual stipulation: If he were to leave for any school other than Alabama, the buyout would be relatively small— $3 million through 2022, $2 million through 2025, and $1 million through 2027. But if he were to bolt for Tuscaloosa, he'd owe the school an additional $1.5 million through 2022, an additional $1 million through 2025, and an additional $500,000 through 2027. This eye-popping proviso reinforced the conception that virtually everything at Clemson was done with the Crimson Tide in the back of the mind.

"I was at Alabama 13 years," Dabo said in 2019. "I love Alabama and always will. That won't change. But I'm going on my 17th year at Clemson, my 11th as head coach. I love where I am, love what I do."

The contract also requires that Dabo be one of the three highest paid coaches in college football after a season in which the Tigers make the playoff semifinals. And if he were not in the top three in this scenario, he would be free to leave for another job—even the one at Alabama—without having to pay a cash penalty. This begs the question: Would Dabo ever pack his bags for Bama if Nick Saban retired and mama called? It's a topic that is debated weekly—both during the season and in the offseason—on sports talk radio stations across Alabama.

"Dabo has it so good at Clemson that I don't think he'd ever leave," said Jay Barker, one of Swinney's former teammates and friends who does a radio show out of Birmingham. "Dabo has built his own kingdom in Clemson and he plays in a conference that isn't as strong as the SEC, so you can almost pencil in Clemson into playoffs each season. Plus, who would want to follow Nick Saban? You always want to be the guy after the guy who follows the legend, not the one who immediately replaces the legend."

"I can't see Dabo leaving Clemson for Alabama," said Antonio Langham, another one of Swinney's former teammates who remains a close friend. "He's got everything he needs up there at Clemson and if he needs something more, they'll give it to him. His life is at Clemson. He raised his kids at Clemson. He's a big part of the Clemson community. Why leave something that is so perfect?"

And yet: Clemson doesn't have nearly the fan following of the Tide, not by a longshot. Of the twenty most watched college football games during the 2019 regular season, not one of them featured Little Ol' Clemson. Then in the ACC championship game, roughly 3.3 million saw the Tigers demolish Virginia; in the SEC championship game played later that day, more than 13 million watched LSU beat Georgia and that night about the same number of viewers flipped on the Big 10 title matchup between Ohio State and Wisconsin.

To Clemson's credit, this lack of overall program star power hasn't had a negative impact on recruiting—a testament to Dabo's persuasion skills. When he became Clemson's full-time head coach in 2010, his first recruiting class ranked twenty-seventh in the country. It featured players who were mostly from the southeast and lived a few hours' drive from the Clemson campus. Ten years later in 2020, Little Ol' Clemson reeled in what was widely regarded as the finest group of recruits in the country, the first time in Tiger history that its incoming class was ranked No. 1. Dabo signed players from virtually every part of the country, from California to Connecticut to Pennsylvania to Florida and in between. One of Clemson's recruiting secrets is that Dabo and his staff have employed social media to communicate their message to recruits as adeptly as any Top 20 program; Clemson's Twitter account has almost as many followers—over 1 million—as any school in the country.

Yet the question remains: Why is Clemson's fan base so miniscule when compared to other elite programs? The population of Clemson—fourteen thousand—is the smallest of any school that has ever participated in the College Football Playoffs. Dabo has joked that the town is big-time because it has a Walmart *and* a Publix grocery store, but there's no denying that it's a different world in small-town Clemson—where time can stand still, where churches outnumber restaurants—than it is where other major universities are. Is Clemson the Duke of college football? Will the Tigers dynasty one day rival the University of Miami's run in 1980s and early 1990s?

As for Clemson's current state? Dabo wouldn't have it any other way. The role of outsider is one that he's been playing to much acclaim for years now.

THE SCENE WAS SO unfamiliar: quarterback Trevor Lawrence, moving from player to player in the Mercedes-Benz Super-dome locker room in New Orleans, consoling his teammates, telling each that he loved him. On January 13, 2020, in Atlanta, LSU beat Clemson 42–25 for the national title, the first time in thirty games that Clemson had lost.

Dabo had a chance to become the fourth head coach in the AP Poll Era, which dated back to 1936, to win three national titles in a four-year span, joining Nick Saban (2009, 2011, 2012); Nebraska's Tom Osborne (1994, 1995, 1997); and Notre Dame's Frank Leahy (1946, 1947, 1949). But he came up one win short.

Not surprisingly, Dabo was as optimistic as ever after the game. He had earlier proclaimed that the 2010s were all about constructing his program and putting the proper building blocks in place. Now he believed the 2020s would be "the roaring twenties" for the Tigers because they were built to last as annual title contenders. "Our guys competed our tails off," Dabo said after the loss to LSU. "This will be a painful tape to watch, but one that will help us. It'll help us get back to work and build next year's team."

But by the end of 2020, things were hardly roaring for Dabo. As Clemson prepared to play Ohio State in its sixth consecutive appearance in the College Football Playoffs—no other team had made every playoff since the format was implemented in 2014—Dabo had become something that a few years earlier seemed unimaginable:

A polarizing figure.

THE SWIRL OF CONTROVERSY surrounding Dabo started just after the coronavirus pandemic gripped the United States. In April 2020, after the National Basketball Association and other major sports leagues shut down competition due to the outbreak of COVID-19, Dabo said he had "zero doubt that we're going to be playing [in the fall] and the stands are going to be packed" and added "we're going to rise up and kick this thing in the teeth and get back to our lives." When asked why he was so confident that the coronavirus would be wiped out in a relatively short duration even though medical experts were warning the pandemic could kill hundreds of thousands, he said, "We've stormed the beaches of Normandy. We've sent a rover out on Mars and walked on the moon."

The media pilloried Dabo, labeling his remarks as ill-informed at best and dangerous at worst. But those who know Dabo best say he was only trying to express optimism and stay upbeat—two of his longtime personality traits—and that he wasn't courting controversy by any measure. But then in June, when professional and college athletes around the nation were protesting racial injustice and police brutality in the wake of the death of George Floyd in Minneapolis, Dabo stood in front of microphones and offered his analysis of what was transpiring. "What I know as I approach everything from a perspective of faith is that where there are people, there's going to be hate, there's going to be racism and greed and jealousy and crime and so on because we live in a fallen world."

Once again, Dabo was hammered in the media. His lack of perceived empathy with a cause that was so near and dear to many of his players—both present and past—was viewed as a verbal slap in the face. Instead of trying to do something about the issue of racism in the United States, he implied that it was an issue that would never go away, no matter what anyone did to combat it. Later, a photograph circulated on Twitter of Dabo wearing a "Football Matters" T-shirt. This was a phrase used as part of an NFL campaign, but some interpreted it as him mocking or belittling the Black Lives Matter movement. The entire episode made him look out of touch with what was important to his players and to millions across the nation, and so did his statement that he didn't like the stickers placed on the Clemson helmets that supported social justice reform, not because he didn't support the movement but because he was a "traditionalist" who didn't want to change the appearance of Clemson's uniform.

He learned his lesson, however. In March 2020, Dabo marched with his players in a display of solidarity for social justice and told reporters, "I'm embarrassed to say that there's things on this campus I didn't really understand. I knew the basics but not the details. But I've learned and I've listened."

FOR THE SIXTH STRAIGHT season in 2020, Clemson advanced to the College Football Playoffs, where the Tigers faced Ohio State in the national semifinals. Due to myriad COVID issues and a late start to the season by the Big 10, the Buckeyes had played only six games, which prompted Dabo to place Ohio State at No. 11 on his final ballot in the coaches' poll. This did not go over well with the Buckeyes players, who viewed it as a massive and purposeful slight.

Dabo never backed down from his vote, explaining that he reserved his Top 10 for teams that had played more than six games. After the Buckeyes manhandled Clemson 49–28 in the Sugar Bowl, Dabo still didn't second-guess himself for ranking Ohio State No. 11. "No, I don't regret any of that," he said. "And polls have nothing to do with motivation."

Still, late in the fourth quarter, Ohio State senior defensive linemen Jonathon Cooper and Haskell Garrett grabbed a whiteboard on the sideline and wrote the number 11. At 12:27 a.m. on January 2—about two hours after the game had ended—Cooper Tweeted: "We were ranked 11th @ClemsonFB."

Whether or not you believe in the value of bulletin board material, it would be hard to imagine Nick Saban—who ten days later would lead the Crimson Tide to its sixth national title in eleven years with a 52–24 victory over Ohio State—doing anything within a country mile that could possibly provoke a potential opponent. Some head coaches tend to be so tight-lipped that their press conferences can devolve into an exercise in the Socratic method—the coach answers a question with a question. But not Dabo. He speaks with no filter, usually an admirable trait, but too often in 2020 it wasn't.

There was more. On November 21, 2020, Clemson was scheduled to play Florida State. In the week leading up to the game, the Tigers had a player—a backup offensive lineman—show mild symptoms of being infected with the coronavirus. He tested negative, however, and was allowed to practice while wearing a mask and maintaining social distance from his teammates. The player was then allowed to travel with the team to Tallahassee, sitting in the back of the plane. On Friday night at the team hotel, the player tested positive for the virus. This prompted Florida State to postpone the game, which detonated Dabo's anger.

"This game was not cancelled because of COVID," Dabo said. "COVID was just an excuse to cancel the game. I have no doubt their players wanted to play and would have played—and same with the coaches. To me, the Florida State administration forfeited the game." Dabo noted that it cost Clemson over $300,000 to make the trip to Florida State.

"That's $300,000 that's gone out the window," he said. "If the standard to play was zero positive tests, we never would've had a season."

"It absolutely was a COVID issue," Florida State's Mike Norvell said after hearing Dabo's comments. "Football coaches are not doctors. Some of us might think we are, but there's a reason why medical advisors make decisions based on the information that is provided."

Dabo wasn't done. Two days after the game was canceled, he said on his radio show, "I don't give a crap what they say. I know what the facts are." Dabo also doesn't give a crap that many disagree with his stance that players shouldn't be paid. He has said that "professionalizing college athletics, that's where you lose me. I'll go do something else, because there's enough entitlement in this world as it is." Dabo believes in the power in education to change lives—just as it did his— but that compensating players would be the death knell for college football, even though he earned more than $8 million in 2020.

Then, later in the fall of 2020, Dabo questioned why the NCAA gave players Election Day off, saying that most of them had already voted. The symbolism of the NCAA's decision— emphasizing the importance of young people voting—was lost on Dabo, whose comments on COVID, George Floyd, and voting all came off as the same thing: tone-deaf.

In a matter of months, Little Ol' Clemson—a program that for years had been known as loveable upstarts led by a folksy, fun-loving coach—had been turned into college football's dark knights. Now the question is: How will Dabo respond, and where does his program go from here?

IN THE 2021 SEASON, quarterback Trevor Lawrence—the top pick in April's NFL draft—will be replaced by D.J. Uiagalelei, the consensus No. 1 pro-style quarterback recruit in the class of 2020. Last season, in Clemson's 47–40 overtime loss to Notre Dame, Uiagalelei threw for more yards (439) against the Irish than any quarterback ever had in the long, storied history of Irish football. Over the last four years, according to Rivals.com, the Tigers' average recruiting class ranking has been 6.25, which is the third highest in the nation over that stretch, trailing only Georgia (2.0) and Alabama (3.25).

By most outward appearances and the inner sanctum of mathematical stats, the football machine and fortunes of Little Ol' Clemson will continue to hum. Is an eighth consecutive national playoff on the horizon? Dabo is betting on it for sure.

As Swinney enters the prime of his coaching career, two coaches in their professional winters see no regression anytime soon at Clemson under Swinney. "They do a great job in recruiting. They do a great job of developing players," said Nick Saban. "That's why we tried to hire Dabo years ago."

"Dabo is going to win more championships at Clemson," said Bruce Arians, the Super Bowl–winning coach of the Tampa Bay Buccaneers who for several years had the same agent as Dabo. "He understands how to connect with players, how to motivate players, and how to teach players. That's the key to coaching—teaching and motivating. Dabo is the full package, man, and I think he's the future of college football. I sure as hell wouldn't want to go head-to-head against him in the next decade or two."

THERE HE WAS, SITTING at his desk in his spacious Clemson office, talking over the phone to a longtime acquaintance in Tuscaloosa in late February 2021. The Tigers had just begun their spring practice, a time for scheming and dreaming, and Dabo liked what he was seeing out of his team, which most college football experts believed would begin the upcoming season ranked No. 1 in the nation and would be the prohibitive favorite to win the national title. A few days earlier, Dabo had quoted a famous politician to express both the challenges that lay ahead and his overall personal coaching philosophy.

"[Winston] Churchill had a quote that I've always loved: 'Success is not infallible. Failure is not fatal It's the courage to continue that counts,'" Dabo said. "I've always believed that. For us, it's continuing to grind, learn, grow, believe and serve. It's always about what's next. That's been our philosophy for a long time. We are excited and hungry to attack this 2021 journey."

Now in his office and talking on the phone, Dabo was in a storytelling mood, as if he were on his front porch in a rocking chair sipping a big ol' glass of sweet tea with an old friend. He spoke with pride about his first play as an Alabama player, a toss-sweep against Southern Miss in 1989, when Dabo was a redshirt freshman. Dabo was blocking a cornerback when he got run over by Tide fullback Martin Houston. "I'd never been so excited to get run over by my own guy in my life," he said.

He recalled tackling the Florida punter on a botched play in the 1992 SEC championship game, resulting in a loss of 13 yards, the most on a single play of the entire national-championship winning season. "Swinney had the biggest sack of the year, not [Derrick] Curry, not [John] Copeland," he said, referring to Alabama's starting All-American defensive ends who wound up being selected in the first round of the NFL draft.

He told the story about how on February 2, 2021, as he and his wife woke up in bed early that morning, she gave him a kiss and said, "Happy hiring day." It had been exactly twenty-five years since Alabama coach Gene Stallings called Dabo—who at that point had recently completed his two years as a graduate assistant coach and was cleaning gutters to earn money while he looked for a job—into his office.

"Sit down, Dabo," Stallings said on February 2, 1996. "I need a young guy on my staff. I want you to coach ends [tight ends and wide receivers]. I'll pay you $38,000 and that's more than you're worth. I'll give you a car. If I hear you got this job before I announce it, you ain't got this job."

A quarter-century later, as Dabo was driving home from the office on February 2, 2021, he phoned Stallings at 5:30 p.m. and thanked him for hiring him all those years ago. During their conversation, Stallings told Dabo that one of his grand-daughters worked in the athletic department at the University of Arizona and was looking for a new job. Dabo quickly realized this was his chance to repay a long-overdue debt.

"When I hang up this phone, I'm going to let her know she's got a job at Clemson," Dabo told Stallings. "Here's what I'm going to pay her and that's way more than she's worth. I know she'll do a good job. If I hear she gets this job before I announce that she's got this job, she won't get this job." Sharing the details of the call as he sat in his office, Dabo laughed at the memory. The tale distilled the essence of the man:

In Dabo's world—a complicated, faith-based place where things aren't always as rosy as they seem—two things are immutable:

Love and loyalty are the keystones of life.

ACKNOWLEDGMENTS

The genesis of this book can be traced to a phone call I had with my friend Richard Deitsch, a former colleague at *Sports Illustrated* who now writes for *The Athletic*. We were talking about potential book ideas when he mentioned the name of Dabo Swinney. "That story is right in your backyard," Deitsch said. After speaking with more writers, my literary agent, and friends that I have in common with Dabo, I grew more intrigued with the idea. Weeks later, I began my quest to understand William Christopher Swinney.

In recent years reporters from around the nation have penned books and detailed stories on Dabo, but I want to especially acknowledge a dozen writers whose works I especially leaned on in crafting this narrative: Manie Robinson, Larry Williams, Seth Davis, Tim Rohan, Dan Wetzel, Kent Babb, Andy Staples, Sam Blackman, Tim Bourret, Bruce Shoenfeld, David M. Hale, and Stewart Mandel.

I'm in debt to so many folks who spoke to me about Dabo— some on the record, some on the condition of anonymity, some providing background only. These interviews provided colorful insight into the life and times of Dabo and those who are closest to him.

My literary agent, Richard Pine, believed in this project from the beginning. My editor at Grand Central Publishing, Sean Desmond, wielded a graceful editing pen and his ideas about structure and pacing were always spot on. Rachel Kambury at Grand Central made sure that deadlines were (mostly) met and patiently answered all of my editing questions. I'm grateful to be surrounded by such a talented, friendly team at Grand Central.

My stepfather, Gordon Bratz, a retired Army colonel and a former professor at West Point, edited an early draft of the manuscript. His deft touches are all over the narrative. He remains my secret writing weapon—and one of my favorite people on the planet. One of Dabo's friends in the Birmingham area, Matt Coulter (a television and radio legend in Alabama), spent hours fact-checking the book; if there are any errors, however, they are mine and mine alone.

Finally, writing books is a solitary process and it often requires extended time away from your family. My kids—Lincoln, 6; Autumn, 4; and Farrah, 4—are my everything. Daddy is officially back on full-time duty.

NOTES

CHAPTER 1: RUN, DABO, RUN

3   **Oh my God:** Dan Wetzel, "Dabo Swinney Emphasized More than X's and O's to Turn Around Clemson," Yahoo! Sports, October 18, 2013, https://sports.yahoo.com/news/ncaaf--dabo-swinney-emphasized-more-than-x-s-and-o-s-to-reserruct-clemson-055947686.html.

4   **Dabo spent many Saturday mornings:** Wetzel, "Dabo Swinney Emphasized More."

4   **He wanted the buses to drive:** Wetzel, "Dabo Swinney Emphasized More."

5   **"Y'all are not listening to me":** Wetzel, "Dabo Swinney Emphasized More."

7   **Pick them up and put them down:** Wetzel, "Dabo Swinney Emphasized More."

CHAPTER 2: A HARD LIFE IN PELHAM

18   **"Uh oh, he's going to be a fighter":** Manie Robinson, *Top of the Hill: Dabo Swinney and Clemson's Rise to College Football Greatness* (Chicago: Triumph Books, 2018), 1.

20   **Dabo became such a presence:** Seth Davis, *Getting to Us: How Great Coaches Make Great Teams* (New York: Penguin Books, 2019), 251.

21   **he'd step to the plate and pivot:** Scott Keepfer, "Dabo Swinney Turns 50," The Greenville News, November 20, 2019, https://www.greenvilleonline.com/story/sports/2019/11/19/

235

clemson-football-coach-dabo-swinney-celebrates-50th-birthday/
2585053001/

21 **"Oh, that's me, isn't it?":** Ron Morris, "Family Matters for Swinney,"
the State, January 10, 2017, https://www.thestate.com/sports/spt-
columns-blogs/ron-morris/article14359523.html.

22 **"Shut up, Peppy!":** Robinson, *Top of the Hill*, 2–3.

23 **When Carol would confront him:** Davis, *Getting to Us*, 253.

26 **Carol stayed upstairs:** Larry Williams, *Clemson Tough: Guts and
Glory Under Dabo Swinney* (Charleston, SC: The History Press,
2016), 17.

28 **"Mama, don't worry":** Davis, *Getting to Us*, 254.

30 **Teachers taught her reading, writing, and arithmetic:** Davis, *Getting
to Us*, 249.

31 **Carol spotted another girl twirling a baton:** Davis, *Getting to Us*, 250.

32 **Kathleen wanted to become:** Will Vandervort, "Kathleen Swinney:
Dabo's First Recruit," Clemson Insider, June 25, 2013, https://
theclemsoninsider.com/2013/06/25/kathleen-swinney-dabos-first-
recruit/.

33 **"You know, I just don't want a girlfriend right now":** Robinson, *Top
of the Hill*, 14–15.

33 **They reignited their romance:** Davis, *Getting to Us*, 252.

33 **Dabo took Kathleen to a restaurant in Hoover:** Robinson, *Top of the
Hill*, 16.

35 **Dabo was so moved by Jones's words:** Birmingham Christian
Family, "Alabama's Tiger: Dabo Swinney," Birmingham Christian
Family, August 26, 2016, https://birminghamchristian.com/
alabamas-tiger-dabo-swinney/.

CHAPTER 3: DEFYING THE ODDS IN TUSCALOOSA

39 **"I can do that":** Williams, *Clemson Tough*, 18.

42 **But the administrator was unmoved:** Davis, *Getting to Us*, 255.

43 **At one point Dabo dropped to his knees:** Davis, *Getting to Us*, 256.

44 **"If you give me your address":** Davis, *Getting to Us*, 256.

44 **"Wait a minute!":** Robinson, *Top of the Hill*, 8.

45 **Dabo yelled in joy:** Davis, *Getting to Us*, 256.

46 **They won't miss me:** David Hood, "Don't Miss Practice: Dabo
Swinney Learns Painful Lesson at Alabama," TigerNet.com, May 16,
2020, https://www.tigernet.com/story/Dont-Miss-Practice-Dabo-
Swinney-learns-painful-lesson-at-Alabama-18796.

47 **"Mr. Swinney," Wingo said, "you will be with me when flex is over":**
Hood, "Don't Miss Practice."

48 **"Mr. Swinney, I want you to come lead us in flex today":** Hood,
"Don't Miss Practice."

49   **"It was a little different at first":** John Talty, "Meet the Man Who Lived with Dabo Swinney and His Mom," AL.com, January 6, 2016, https://www.al.com/alabamafootball/2016/01/meet_the_man_who_lived_with_da.html.

49   **But the best times were on Sunday nights:** Davis, *Getting to Us*, 257.

52   **"Men," he said, "I guarantee you will win":** Ken Rogers, "Bill Curry Recalls the Brick," Dothan Eagle, November 17, 2010, https://dothaneagle.com/sports/bill-curry-recalls-the-brick/article_c988149d-d206-527f-971d-db6f902b8310.html.

54   **He wondered if he missed a block:** Robinson, *Top of the Hill*, 9.

54   **McCorvey later said that Dabo always did things "correctly":** Davis, *Getting to Us*, 258.

54   **"Dab, I need somebody who can catch the football":** Robinson, *Top of the Hill*, 9–10.

54   **Dabo took off running to the locker room:** Davis, *Getting to Us*, 258.

55   **He framed it:** Davis, *Getting to Us*, 259.

63   **One man whose gutters he worked on:** Williams, *Clemson Tough*, 19.

63   **Until that moment, Dabo had never seriously considered:** Davis, *Getting to Us*, 259.

64   **"This is the ring I want":** Andrea Adelson, "The Making of Dabo Swinney's Clemson Tigers Family," ESPN.com, December 30, 2015, https://www.espn.com/blog/acc/post/_/id/89870/growing-up-with-dabo-the-making-of-a-family-man.

65   **Happy Valentine's Day to my #1 V'tine!:** Robinson, *Top of the Hill*, 19–20.

67   **In January 2001, the *Commercial Appeal* in Memphis:** Robinson, *Top of the Hill*, 22.

CHAPTER 4: DABO IN WILDERNESS

71   **"I really just went to meet him":** Jon Solomon, "Dabo's Lost Years," cbssports.com, December 21, 2015, https://www.cbssports.com/college-football/news/dabos-lost-years-how-clemsons-swinney-got-back-into-coaching/.

72   **Wingo then told his former player:** Kent Babb, "Dabo Swinney Was the Best Shopping Center Leasing Agent in Alabama," *Washington Post*, November 5, 2015.

72   **He had no clue what he was getting himself into:** Williams, *Clemson Tough*, 20.

73   **This woman wanted to thank Dabo:** Larry Williams, *Dabo's Dynasty: Clemson's Rise to College Football Supremacy* (Charleston, SC: The History Press, 2019), 103.

73 **seeing Dabo go off to work:** Williams, *Clemson Tough*, 20.

73 **Once Dabo arrived at the AIG Baker office:** Babb, "Best Shopping Center Leasing Agent in Alabama."

74 **He attended shopping center conventions:** Babb, "Best Shopping Center Leasing Agent in Alabama."

75 **every time he walked into a meeting:** Babb, "Best Shopping Center Leasing Agent in Alabama."

76 **"You know you're sitting here":** Babb, "Best Shopping Center Leasing Agent in Alabama."

78 **Dabo didn't realize it at the time:** Babb, "Best Shopping Center Leasing Agent in Alabama."

79 **At intersections, on vacant lots:** Babb, "Best Shopping Center Leasing Agent in Alabama."

80 **"I have all this knowledge of football":** Williams, *Clemson Tough*, 21.

81 **"You're never going to believe where I am!":** Williams, *Dabo's Dynasty*, 10.

82 **the pressure to succeed in football:** Davis, *Getting to Us*, 261.

83 **"Why me?" Dabo asked:** Babb, "Best Shopping Center Leasing Agent in Alabama."

84 **"No," Dabo said. "What do you think about moving to Clemson?":** Williams, *Dabo's Dynasty*, 103.

86 **Once he got Dabo on the phone:** Babb, "Best Shopping Center Leasing Agent in Alabama."

87 **Today the sign CALL DABO SWINNEY hangs in his garage:** Babb, "Best Shopping Center Leasing Agent in Alabama."

CHAPTER 5: DABO COMES BACK TO CAROLINA

88 **On this day, Pearman, now an offensive tackles coach:** Williams, *Dabo's Dynasty*, 17.

89 **"Make sure you look over there":** Williams, *Dabo's Dynasty*, 18.

91 **Some of the wide receivers believed:** Chansi Stuckey, "Dabo Swinney Yelled and Screamed and Turned Me into an NFL Wide Receiver," Vice, September 21, 2017, https://www.vice.com/en/article/qvjv37/dabo-swinney-yelled-and-screamed-and-turned-me-into-an-nfl-wide-receiver.

92 **His two older boys sometimes attended practices:** Robinson, *Top of the Hill*, 29–30.

93 **He told his wife, "Kath, I can't do this anymore":** Robinson, *Top of the Hill*, 29–30.

93 **"Listen," Dabo said, "I just want y'all to know":** Robinson, *Top of the Hill*, 29–30.

94 **He started bringing them around the office:** Robinson, *Top of the Hill*, 29–30.

96   **"I don't know if we're getting fired":** Williams, *Dabo's Dynasty*, 102.

96   **Clemson athletic director Terry Don Phillips had essentially decided:** Williams, *Dabo's Dynasty*, 101.

98   **I want to make sure you're going to follow through:** Williams, *Dabo's Dynasty*, 68.

99   **"I'm about 99 percent sure I'm coming to Clemson":** Robinson, *Top of the Hill*, 33–34.

100   **"Listen," Bowden said, "are you coming to Clemson?":** Williams, *Dabo's Dynasty*, 66–67.

101   **"You just bloom where you're planted":** Williams, *Dabo's Dynasty*, 69.

103   **Dabo was ready to accept the offer:** Williams, *Dabo's Dynasty*, 103.

104   **But then he received a phone call:** Williams, *Dabo's Dynasty*, 104.

105   **"I had associate head coach [available]":** Andy Staples, "No Ordinary Interim: How Dabo Swinney Turned a Seven-Week Job into a Clemson Dynasty," SI, October 10, 2018, https://www.si.com/college/2018/10/10/dabo-swinney-tommy-bowden-interim-2008-clemson.

106   **he had promised the first carry of the season:** Staples, "No Ordinary Interim."

107   **Kathleen Swinney walked out of the Georgia Dome:** Vandervort, "Kathleen Swinney: Dabo's First Recruit."

CHAPTER 6: THE HEAD COACH

109   **"Well, why don't we just make a change now?":** Sam Blackman and Tim Bourette, *If These Walls Could Talk: Clemson Tigers* (Chicago: Triumph Books, 2016), 3.

109   **He'd been paying close attention to Dabo:** Staples, "No Ordinary Interim."

110   **"Dabo, you're in charge":** Staples, "No Ordinary Interim."

110   **What is going to happen to us?:** Vandervort, "Kathleen Swinney: Dabo's First Recruit."

111   **"We're okay":** Vandervort, "Kathleen Swinney: Dabo's First Recruit."

111   **of the previous twenty-nine coaches in major college football:** Staples, "No Ordinary Interim."

112   **"I want you to know that I've watched you":** Williams, *Dabo's Dynasty*, 123.

112   **"Here's what I want you to do":** Williams, *Dabo's Dynasty*, 124.

115   **"None of you owe me anything":** Blackman and Bourette, *If These Walls Could Talk*, 5.

115   **Dabo quickly replied that Bear:** Ron Morris, "Making Business Sense of Dabo Swinney," *Charlotte Observer*, December 2, 2015.

117   **Man, this is real:** Williams, *Dabo's Dynasty*, 122.

117   **"You're not going to believe this":** Williams, *Dabo's Dynasty*, 122.

118   **for years, he declined to go into the harsh details:** Davis, *Getting to Us*, 269.

119   **"Sir, I do not want to be disrespectful":** Robinson, *Top of the Hill*, 45 –46.

120   **The binder contains every imaginable football subject:** Davis, *Getting to Us*, 267.

120   **For years he had bounced ideas off her:** Vandervort, "Kathleen Swinney: Dabo's First Recruit."

121   **When he reached midfield, Dabo slowed:** Bruce Schoenfeld, "How Dabo Swinney Turned Clemson Football into a Juggernaut," *New York Times*, January 10, 2020.

122   **"You'd have thought we'd won the national championship":** Staples, "No Ordinary Interim."

124   **"That's the thing I wanted to make sure of":** Chris Low, "Meet the Man Who Always Believed in Dabo Swinney," ESPN.com, January 9, 2017, https://www.espn.com/college-football/story/_/id/18441434/clemson-tigers-dabo-swinney-national-champion-thanks-man-hired-believed-him.

125   **"Had I not been prepared to be a head coach":** Staples, "No Ordinary Interim."

127   **Dabo even circled the two words of advice:** SI Staff, "P.A.W. Patrol," SI.com, November 16, 2015, https://vault.si.com/vault/2015/11/16/paw-patrol.

127   **"No! If you are asking me, it's a pretty good bet":** Robinson, *Top of the Hill*, 49–50.

128   **Most everyone in college football circles knew that Saban:** Ray Glier, *How the SEC Became Goliath: The Making of College Football's Most Dominant Conference* (New York: Howard Books, 2013), 195–203.

130   **Every summer Dabo gathered his staff:** Davis, *Getting to Us*, 268.

130   **During the retreat, the coaches discuss:** David M. Hale, "The Tao of Dabo Swinney," ESPN.com, December 31, 2017, https://www.espn.com/college-football/story/_/id/21916855/clemson-tigers-dabo-swinney-culture-alabama-crimson-tide-nick-saban-process.

131   **Many of Dabo's favorite phrases:** Hale, "The Tao of Dabo Swinney."

CHAPTER 7: THE BUILDING OF DABO'S DYNASTY

137   **On the day of his visit to Boyd's home:** Robinson, *Top of the Hill*, 85 –86.

138   **Dabo watched from under an umbrella:** Robinson, *Top of the Hill*, 97–98.

140 **"Sit down":** Robinson, *Top of the Hill*, 72.

141 **Dabo called Gus Malzahn:** Robinson, *Top of the Hill*, 81.

142 **"There are a lot of teams in this country":** Robinson, *Top of the Hill*, 79–80.

143 **He'd never had much sympathy:** Dan Wetzel, "Dabo Swinney Travels Long Road to Restore Clemson to Prominence," Yahoo! Sports, September 19, 2012, https://sports.yahoo.com/news/ncaaf--dabo-swinney-travels-long-road-to-restore-clemson-to-prominence.html.

143 **"20 something years he just threw his life away":** Wetzel, "Dabo Swinney Travels Long Road."

143 **Dabo told his brother he would:** Wetzel, "Dabo Swinney Travels Long Road."

144 **On a Friday night before Clemson played:** Michael Bamberger, "Reborn in Death Valley," SI.com, October 31, 2011, https://vault.si.com/vault/2011/10/31/reborn-in-death-valley.

145 **"Hey look, do with [Brent's number] what you want":** Williams, *Dabo's Dynasty*, 81.

146 **"No, you don't get to bring nobody":** Williams, *Dabo's Dynasty*, 82.

147 **The *Washington Post* headline over a story:** Davis, *Getting to Us*, 264.

148 **Dabo grabbed a pen and sketched a grand football facility:** Schoenfeld, "How Dabo Swinney Turned Clemson Football."

149 **if Dabo could convince Hendrix:** Schoenfeld, "How Dabo Swinney Turned Clemson Football."

149 **Hendrix guided Dabo to the back porch:** Schoenfeld, "How Dabo Swinney Turned Clemson Football."

150 **Dabo asked Hendrix if he saw Clemson win:** Schoenfeld, "How Dabo Swinney Turned Clemson Football."

150 **"Well," Dabo said, jabbing himself in the chest:** Schoenfeld, "How Dabo Swinney Turned Clemson Football."

150 **"When I got this job, everybody talked":** Williams, *Clemson Tough*, 75.

151 **The entire payroll for the miniscule support staff:** Davis, *Getting to Us*, 264.

151 **When Clemson coaches asked them why:** SI Staff, "Learning to Fly," SI.com, January 16, 2017, https://vault.si.com/vault/2017/01/16/learning-fly.

152 **On Mondays, he meets with a leadership group:** Davis, *Getting to Us*, 266.

153 **"He can just talk and talk forever":** Davis, *Getting to Us*, 246.

153 **"When you say it enough so your players repeat it":** Davis, *Getting to Us*, 264.

153 **Once the movie is over, a staffer:** Davis, *Getting to Us*, 265.

155 **The Watsons were handed the keys:** Robinson, *Top of the Hill*, 120–122.

157   **When Big Erv moved back to Birmingham:** SI Staff, "P.A.W. Patrol."

158   **The good Lord can take me right now:** Brian Hamilton, "You Don't Know Dabo," SI.com, November 3, 2015, https://www.si.com/college/2015/11/03/clemsons-dabo-swinney-colorful-charismatic-new-king-football-south-carolina.

160   **Dabo saw a piece of grass growing in a crack:** SI Staff, "P.A.W. Patrol."

162   **Father and son had a ritual:** Aaron Brenner, "Swinney Finds Peace After Father's Passing," *Post and Courier*, December 28, 2015.

163   **And yet there still was a kind of hollowness:** Brenner, "Swinney Finds Peace."

164   **The defense was a reflection of their coach:** SI Staff, "On the Outside Looking Up," SI.com, January 11, 2016, https://vault.si.com/vault/2016/01/11/outside-looking.

166   **"We ain't no underdogs":** SI Staff, "On the Outside."

166   **how much he admired Bear Bryant:** Williams, *Clemson Tough*, 128.

166   **"the rednecks who moved into a nice neighborhood":** SI Staff, "On the Outside."

166   **"This is a matchup [Dabo has] always wanted":** Williams, *Clemson Tough*, 128.

168   **"I'm sorry we didn't get it done":** Williams, *Clemson Tough*, 137.

168   **He got into bed and turned on the television:** Davis, *Getting to Us*, 250–251.

CHAPTER 8: RELIGION, RECRUITING, AND THE RIGHT-HAND MAN

171   **When Dabo arrived at Clemson:** Tim Rohan, "Faith, Football and the Fervent Religious Culture at Dabo Swinney's Clemson," SI.com, September 4, 2019, https://www.si.com/college/2019/09/04/clemson-dabo-swinney-religion-culture.

171   **his relationship with the Lord was the reason:** Rohan, "Faith, Football and the Fervent Religious Culture."

172   **"Have you ever thought about giving":** Rohan, "Faith, Football and the Fervent Religious Culture."

175   **"We thank of the good Lord for the privilege":** Bamberger, "Reborn in Death Valley."

175   **"What I experienced under Coach Swinney":** Bamberger, "Reborn in Death Valley."

176   **Still in his uniform and pads:** Rohan, "Faith, Football and the Fervent Religious Culture."

176   **By April 2014, the Freedom From Religion Foundation:** Rohan, "Faith, Football and the Fervent Religious Culture."

177 **"You just knew that that's something that was important to him":** Ralph Russo, "Keeping the Faith: At Clemson, Religion, Football Converge," AP, December 24, 2015, https://apnews.com/article/8769515d3e9443a787655dc5021fa644.

177 **"We all have our beliefs":** Rohan, "Faith, Football, and the Fervent Religious Culture."

178 **From 2013 to 2015, one former player estimated:** Rohan, "Faith, Football and the Fervent Religious Culture."

179 **"We're going to win some games and lose some games":** Rohan, "Faith, Football and the Fervent Religious Culture."

181 **"Thad, I don't care what you do":** Matt Fortuna, "Many Roles for Clemson's Thad Turnipseed," *New York Times*, January 4, 2017.

181 **"We're going to Clemson, aren't we?":** Ed McGranahan, "It's Not Disney World, but Clemson's New Football Complex Is Close in 'Wow' Factor," *The State*, January 28, 2017.

182 **"Just a totally different atmosphere at Clemson":** Fortuna, "Many Roles for Clemson's Thad Turnipseed."

183 **At first Turnipseed worried that Dabo was too nice:** Hale, "The Tao of Dabo Swinney."

CHAPTER 9: DABO'S FIRST TITLE

184 **The penalty for these minor indiscretions:** SI Staff, "Learning to Fly."

186 **Dabo chose the word *love*:** Davis, *Getting to Us*, 247.

186 **"That's just something that was put on my spirit":** Davis, *Getting to Us*, 247

187 **what made Clemson special:** Robinson, *Top of the Hill*, 211.

188 **"Prosperity is a terrible teacher":** SI Staff, "Case for . . . Clemson," SI.com, December 12, 2016, https://vault.si.com/vault/2016/12/12/case-clemson.

190 **How do you eat an elephant?:** SI Staff, "Learning to Fly."

190 **Dabo learned that Alabama's coach:** SI Staff, "The Imitation Game," SI.com, December 25, 2017, https://vault.si.com/vault/2017/12/25/imitation-game.

192 **"Jay, you love Deshaun, right?":** Davis, *Getting to Us*, 247–248.

192 **"Guys, we know we're good enough":** Davis, *Getting to Us*, 247–248.

195 **"I gotta take a shower. Tell the bus not to leave me":** Ryan McGee, "After the Title, Moments and Chaos and Magic for Dabo Swinney," ESPN.com, January 9, 2017, https://www.espn.com/college-football/story/_/id/18443614/a-most-magical-night-dabo-swinney-celebrating-clemson-tigers-national-championship.

CHAPTER 10: EXTRAVAGANT DREAMING

198   **"There's not a lot of people in this world":** Robinson, *Top of the Hill*, xii–xiii.

199   **Outside the complex:** Robinson, *Top of the Hill*, 246.

200   **"The mindset of this building has always been":** Scott Keepfer, "New Facility, 'Dabo Slide' Set to Open Early Next Year," *Greenville News*, August 13, 2016.

201   **Studying the science of sleep:** Grace Raynor, "Here's How Clemson Football Uses Science to Ensure Its Players Get a Good Night's Sleep," PostandCourier.com, December 16, 2017, https://www.postandcourier.com/sports/heres-how-clemson-football-uses-science-to-ensure-its-players-get-a-good-nights-sleep/article_9ec93a26-e0db-11e7-aa5c-d3905a2c3ac8.html.

202   **If a player struggled to sleep well:** Raynor, "Here's How Clemson Football Uses Science."

206   **According to defensive lineman Clelin Ferrell:** Jordan James, "Dabo Swinney: Clemson Went to Bathroom vs. Bama but Didn't Wipe," 247sports, January 7, 2019, https://247sports.com/Article/Alabama-Clemson-national-championship-Dabo-Swinney-bathroom-story-127455538/.

214   **"To be successful, you have to have a vision":** SI Staff, "The Tide Has Turned," SI.com, January 14, 2019, https://vault.si.com/vault/2019/01/14/tide-has-turned.

214   **So Dabo guided his wife and other family members:** Williams, *Dabo's Dynasty*, 15.

215   **"I've kind of got my own little world":** Dan Wolken, "As Stakes Get Higher in Clemson-Alabama Rivalry, Saban and Swinney Have Grown Closer," *USA Today*, January 6, 2019.

216   **"Dabo is better than Nick at disconnecting":** Wolken, "Saban and Swinney Have Grown Closer."

216   **They've played golf together:** Tim Rohan, "The Vacation Town Where Nick Saban and Dabo Swinney Go to Disappear," SI.com, May 7, 2019, https://www.si.com/college/2019/05/07/nick-saban-dabo-swinney-boca-grande-vacation-contract.

216   **Saban called Dabo and made him a bet:** Rohan, "The Vacation Town."

217   **"Kevin," Dabo said, "that was the best meal I've ever had":** Rohan, "The Vacation Town."

CHAPTER 11: THE FUTURE OF LITTLE OL' CLEMSON

218 **the Tigers had never seized the country's imagination:** Stewart Mandel, "Figuring Out the Mystery of Little Ol' Clemson," the Athletic, January 9, 2020, https://theathletic.com/1520803/2020/01/09/mandel-figuring-out-the-mystery-of-little-ol-clemson/.

219 **One afternoon early in the summer of 2016:** David M. Hale, "How Dabo Swinney Is Influencing the Next Generation of Coaches," ESPN.com, September 19, 2019, https://www.espn.com/college-football/story/_/id/27631731/how-dabo-swinney-influencing-next-generation-coaches.

220 **"You don't know me from Adam":** Hale, "How Dabo Swinney Is Influencing the Next Generation of Coaches."

222 **Of the twenty most watched college football games:** Mandel, "Figuring Out the Mystery."

222 **One of Clemson's recruiting secrets:** Mandel, "Figuring Out the Mystery."

223 **Dabo has joked that the town is big-time:** Mandel, "Figuring Out the Mystery."

226 **"I'm embarrassed to say":** Dan Wolken, "What Happened to Dabo Swinney?" *USA Today*, December 30, 2020.

230 **There he was, sitting at his desk:** Ryan Fowler, *The Game with Ryan Fowler*, Tide 100.9, February 26, 2021, https://soundcloud.com/wdgm-tuscaloosa-tide-99-1/the-game-dabo-swinney-friday-february-26-2021/.

231 **"I'd never been so excited to get run over by my own guy":** Fowler, *The Game with Ryan Fowler.*

INDEX

Index

Index

INDEX

ABOUT THE AUTHOR

LARS ANDERSON is a *New York Times* best-selling author of ten books, including *The Mannings, The Storm and the Tide, Carlisle vs. Army,* and *The All Americans.* A twenty-year veteran of *Sports Illustrated* and a former senior writer at *Bleacher Report,* Anderson is an instructor of journalism at the University of Alabama. He lives in Birmingham, Alabama.

Twitter handle: @LarsAnderson71